How to R...... ...ur

New Puppy
in a Cat Family

The Complete Guide to a Happy, Pet-Filled Home

By

Jackie Sonnenberg

How to Raise Your New Puppy in a Cat Family: The Complete Guide to a Happy, Pet-Filled Home

Copyright © 2011 by Atlantic Publishing Group, Inc.

1405 SW 6th • Ocala, Florida 34471 • 800-814-1132 • Fax 352-622-1875

Web site: www.atlantic-pub.com • E-mail sales@atlantic-pub.com

SAN Number: 268-1250

Library of Congress Cataloging-in-Publication Data

Sonnenberg, Jackie, 1984-
  How to raise your new puppy in a cat family : the complete guide to a happy, pet-filled home / by Jackie Sonnenberg.
    p. cm.
  Includes bibliographical references and index.
  ISBN-13: 978-1-60138-401-0 (alk. paper)
  ISBN-10: 1-60138-401-7 (alk. paper)
  1. Dogs--Training. 2. Cats--Training. 3. Dogs--Health. 4. Cats--Health. 5. Dogs--Behavior. 6. Cats--Behavior. 7. Family life. I. Title.
  SF431.S184 2010
  636.7'0887--dc22

                          2010009335

Printed on Recycled Paper

We recently lost our beloved pet "Bear," who was not only our best and dearest friend but also the "Vice President of Sunshine" here at Atlantic Publishing. He did not receive a salary but worked tirelessly 24 hours a day to please his parents. Bear was a rescue dog that turned around and showered myself, my wife, Sherri, his grandparents Jean, Bob, and Nancy, and every person and animal he met (maybe not rabbits) with friendship and love. He made a lot of people smile every day.

We wanted you to know that a portion of the profits of this book will be donated to The Humane Society of the United States. —*Douglas & Sherri Brown*

The human-animal bond is as old as human history. We cherish our animal companions for their unconditional affection and acceptance. We feel a thrill when we glimpse wild creatures in their natural habitat or in our own backyard.

Unfortunately, the human-animal bond has at times been weakened. Humans have exploited some animal species to the point of extinction.

The Humane Society of the United States makes a difference in the lives of animals here at home and worldwide. The HSUS is dedicated to creating a world where our relationship with animals is guided by compassion. We seek a truly humane society in which animals are respected for their intrinsic value, and where the human-animal bond is strong.

Want to help animals? We have plenty of suggestions. Adopt a pet from a local shelter, join the HSUS and be a part of our work to help companion animals and wildlife. You will be funding our educational, legislative, investigative and outreach projects in the U.S. and across the globe.

Or perhaps you'd like to make a memorial donation in honor of a pet, friend or relative? You can through our Kindred Spirits program. And if you'd like to contribute in a more structured way, our Planned Giving Office has suggestions about estate planning, annuities, and even gifts of stock that avoid capital gains taxes.

Maybe you have land that you would like to preserve as a lasting habitat for wildlife. Our Wildlife Land Trust can help you. Perhaps the land you want to share is a backyard—that's enough. Our Urban Wildlife Sanctuary Program will show you how to create a habitat for your wild neighbors.

So you see, it's easy to help animals. And the HSUS is here to help.

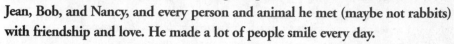

THE HUMANE SOCIETY
OF THE UNITED STATES.

2100 L Street NW • Washington, DC 20037 • 202-452-1100
www.hsus.org

DEDICATION

I dedicate this to my own late fur ball

Roscoe, "Skeeter," a kid's best friend.

TABLE OF CONTENTS

CHAPTER 2: Before You Choose a Puppy .. 33

CHAPTER 3: Preparing for the Puppy 55

CHAPTER 4: The Language of Cats and Dogs .. 99

CHAPTER 8:
The Health of Your Cat and Puppy 193

CHAPTER 9:
House-training Your Puppy 233

CHAPTER 10: Tips for a Troubled Pair 263

Resources 271

Bibliography 275

Author's Bio 283

Index 285

INTRODUCTION

Hello, cat owner! So, you are thinking about bringing a new puppy home but are concerned your cat will not be very pleased with this new furry friend. Maybe you are worried the puppy will not like your cat; or worse, it will like it too much and want to chase it around the house. Do not worry — many cats and dogs live peacefully under the same roof and even enjoy each other's company. This book will walk you through the steps of choosing and purchasing a new puppy, preparing your cat for a new roommate, introducing the animals using various methods, and organizing day-to-day life with a cat and dog in mind. All of the given scenarios, topics, and information — as well as the insight from pet professionals and everyday people who have done it successfully — will provide you with the confidence and security needed to create a happy, harmonious pet family.

Every cat and dog has a unique personality, not to mention underlining feline and canine characteristics that will dictate their interactions. By explaining the root of these differences, this book will help ease the stress on you and your pets — because once you understand the nature of cats and dogs, you will know how to respond to most problems you encounter.

Of course, this book is based on the premise that you are the owner of a least one cat, and that you are adopting or purchasing a puppy. If you have more than one cat, it is doubtful all of your cats will react in the same manner, so you may have to make special accommodations for each feline. If you are adopting an older dog, most of the advice in this book will still hold true; you may just have to work a bit harder to change the dog's undesirable habits. Even if you already have your new canine addition at home, it is not too late to implement this information. Perhaps you are looking to solve a specific problem — this book will still give you all the advice you need. You might just wish you had picked it up earlier.

The process of finding the right puppy and acclimating it to your home can take months. You must have patience and be consistent when training to be successful. Sure, conflicts will arise, and caring for your two different pets is not a low-maintenance task. However, it is very rare that well-trained cats and dogs cannot be taught how to get along. This book is the first step to a harmonious, multi-pet family — time to get started!

CHAPTER 1

Dispelling the Myths about Cats and Dogs

Ever wonder why many people use the expression, "fighting like cats and dogs"? Many dogs have the natural instinct to "prey drive," and these dogs could regard cats as something small and furry to chase or herd. Wild dogs have the natural instinct to chase small, furry creatures that look like prey. Cats are not the natural prey of dogs, so while a dog may chase or even kill a cat, it will probably not eat it. Human training has caused this instinct to be bred out of many domestic dogs, so the desire to do so is no longer prevalent. . Still, there are differences between breeds that make some more suitable to live with a feline companion.

To successfully introduce a new puppy into a home with a cat, you must understand the truths about cat and dog instincts and behaviors to know how your pets will react to each other. This chapter will examine ten common myths about cats and dogs and explain why they are myths. Once these myths are dispelled, you can begin the process of training yourself to care for these two unique creatures under the same roof. It is no wonder that people often use the cliché, "fighting like cats and dogs," to describe people clashing and having arguments. This cliché feeds into the belief that cats and dogs fight all the time. This brings us to the first myth.

Myth No. 1: Cats and Dogs are Natural Enemies

Think back to Saturday morning cartoons or movies that feature cats and dogs. How did the animals interact? Most often the big, burly dog chases the cat as they growl and hiss at each other until the cat finds a means of escape, like a tall tree. These scenes show stereotypes of cats and dogs, and we forget that they are exaggerated for entertainment purposes. With the proper training and discipline, these two animals can learn to become friends and debunk the myth that cats and dogs are only hostile toward each other.

> **"The most common myth about cats and dogs is that they are polar opposites of each other, and that in order to have both species, you are resigning yourself to conflict between them."**
>
> **— Sassafras Lowrey, pet owner**

> "The first myth is that cats and dogs cannot get along or that you cannot introduce a dog into a cat family. This is false. I do not think that there are any 'facts' about dogs and cats not getting along. In my experience, if done correctly, they can get along. I do not know of any facts that prove that they cannot get along."
>
> **— Debbie Margerum, pet owner**

> "Despite rumors, cats and dogs can get along, and often do get along, extremely well."
>
> **— Dr. Babette Gladstein, DVM**

> "I still hear that dogs and cats fight naturally, which is not true with all dogs and cats. Every single dog can be taught to get along with a cat."
>
> **— Nickey Marriott, owner and proprietor of Doggie Haven Bed and Breakfast**

Pet owners must realize that cats and dogs were once wild animals and have been domesticated over thousands of years. Domestication is the process of humans taking over the care of a species of an animal or plant, which alters natural behaviors such as breeding or diet. Wild dogs have the natural instinct to chase small, furry creatures that look like their prey. However, cats are not the natural prey of dogs, so while a dog may occasionally chase or even kill a cat, it will not eat it. Humans have bred this instinct to chase out of many domesticated dogs, or toned it down considerably; although, in some breeds, this instinct has been enhanced, so it is important to make an educated choice regarding your new puppy's breed. *This will be discussed more in Chapter 2.*

Case Study: Saturday Morning Cartoons

Eric Margerum, pet owner
Vincennes, Indiana

Myth #1: Cats and Dogs are Natural Enemies

When Eric Margerum thought back to his first images of cats and dogs, the first picture that came to his mind was Saturday morning cartoons. The image consisted of a fight between cats and dogs. He describes how the cartoons depicted cats and dogs fighting a lot because of the time period. Many of those older cartoons reflected a time and place where neighborhood cats roamed freely and dogs were usually kept outdoors. When a cat and dog saw each other in cartoons, it was only natural that they got into fights defending territory or following hunting instincts. This also provided entertainment for the audience. Margerum believed that even though these cartoons reflected the time period they were made in, they still reflected natural instincts that animals have. His dog and cat chase each other around his house today to display these natural instincts, but they do not have the intent to cause harm.

Myth No. 2:
A Dog Will Always Win a Fight with a Cat

When most people are asked to think of a cat and dog together, they think of a small cat next to a large dog. This is not always the case, as there are many breeds of dog that are the same size or even smaller than the typical cat, such as a Chihuahua or miniature dachshund. Size may play a part in what type of relationship they have, but the personalities of both animals is more important. Because many breeds of both these animals are relatively similar in size, a dog may not always win a fight with a cat. The two animals may very well be of equal size and strength; therefore, either animal has a chance to cause harm.

Because animals need adequate living space, they may feel threatened when they share the same space with another animal. This can lead to confrontations, but often these are just displays of power that will pass once each animal learns it is not in danger. You must help your pets get through this process safely. Dogs often show aggressive behavior as a form of play. A new puppy will probably try to instigate some roughhousing with the cat, and the cat will not understand the puppy just wants to play. These miscommunications between species can be handled with training once the owner understands how each animal is trying to express itself.

Some dogs may be bullies, but some cats can be bullies too and may display forms of aggression toward the new puppy. The introduction between the puppy and the cat may be one that exemplifies these differences in personalities. The cat, being older and already an established member in the family, can take advantage of a younger puppy and swipe and hiss at it to show the puppy that it is in charge. Many times, dogs may learn to be fearful or spiteful toward the cat, therefore not always coming out as the winners in the cat-and-dog feud.

Play can still turn into a dangerous situation, so take caution if you bring home a large breed. Puppies grow quickly and may not be aware of how much bigger they have become or how to handle their size. Since they are young, they might think that they are smaller than they really are. Discouraging rough play will help a bigger dog learn how to properly and safely play with the cat. This will protect both animals from harm. Do not underestimate the cat's ability to hurt a dog, even if it is larger than the dog. Cats' sharp claws can easily scratch a cute wet nose or big brown eyes.

Myth No. 3:
Cats are Antisocial and Prefer to be Alone

Some people believe that cats prefer to be on their own, as well as be the only pet in the owner's life. Some people believe that cats only prefer to be with other cats and do not like other animals. However, if this were so, they would not make good pets. Cats are friendly and social animals and believe it or not, they can find great companionship with a new puppy.

Cats love to relax and are often content on their own. Sometimes they enjoy being a spectator on the scene instead of being active and involved. People often personify this behavior and think cats are haughty or antisocial, when in reality, most cats prefer to choose when they want that attention, not necessarily when their owners want to give it. Cats do like their alone time but also need attention and love just like any other living thing. Just as people have different personalities, cats are known for having unique personalities — as a cat owner you have no doubt noticed your cat's quirks, which are often quite entertaining. So, your cat may have a shy personality or a rambunctious one. Much of this depends on the breed of the cat and the environment in which it was raised. Sometimes, cats run away and hide when new people they do not know visit the home. This could mean that they are afraid of people they do not know, but they will come out when they are ready to meet the new guests. Sometimes, guests may frighten your cat without meaning to. Cats do not like bold approaches, so if your guests exclaim "Hi kitty! Come here!" in a loud voice with arms outstretched, your cat may think this is an aggressive display. Instead, tell your guests to ignore your cat until it pays them attention.

A cat adopted from a shelter may be more skittish than others. It may have come from the streets or an abusive home and may not have had any positive relationships with humans. Such a cat must learn the skills that other cats learned as small kittens. It is not used to positive attention and may be afraid of being touched. Getting this cat to come out of its shell and learn to like positive attention will be time-consuming and requires patient efforts from the new owners. This old behavior can easily come back if the cat becomes frightened, such as when a new puppy comes into the picture. Take extra care with a cat from these conditions; use the same steps you used to get your shelter cat to know a loving home when introducing the puppy as a new friend.

Myth No. 4:
One Animal is Smarter than the Other

Like parents arguing over whose child is more talented, pet owners often argue about whether cats or dogs are the more intelligent creatures. Of course, a person's personal bias typically leans toward his or her pet of choice. Dog owners may say dogs are smarter because they can better understand their owners and listen to commands, while cat owners may say cats are smarter because they are cautious and more independent. Both animals are intelligent, but they are different species and cannot be compared to each other.

Cats are able to take charge and be independent, which are both trademark signs of intelligence. Notice how a cat will reach under the oven in an attempt to retrieve a wayward toy. To a less-intelligent creature, such as a bear, the toy would be "out of sight, out of mind." An even more amazing display of cat intelligence was noted by attorney and research scientist J. Justin Lancaster. Lancaster adopted Sasha as a stray. His daughter's cotton hair ties were winding up in Sasha's water dish. Then one day Lancaster caught Sasha taking a hair tie from the bathroom; he followed her and saw that she was using the cotton material to absorb the water and then place it on her dry cat food to moisten it. This story may bring to mind some stories of your own cat using "tools" to get what it wants. This indicates advanced intelligence.

Many people think that dogs possess higher intelligence because of their ability to listen to commands and do tricks. Prominent canine researcher Stanley Coren, Ph.D., believes that most dogs are about as intelligent as a 2-year-old child; they can memorize more than 150 words, some more than 250, and even recognize numbers up to five. Coren separates dog intelligence into three categories: instinctive or breed-related intelligence, adaptive or problem-solving abilities, and working and obedience intelligence:

- **Instinctive or breed-related:** What the dog was bred to do.

- **Adaptive or problem-solving:** A dog's ability to solve problems.

- **Working and obedience:** A dog's obedience and working skills, which relate to how quickly it learns.

Some breeds tend to be "smarter" than others. Border collies, poodles, and German shepherds lead the list, while golden retrievers, Doberman pinschers, Shetland sheepdogs, and Labrador retrievers also get high marks for intelligence.

Myth No. 5: Only Dogs Can be Trained

Dogs seem to have a need to please their owners, which is why people can train dogs to do tricks, as well as the basics of potty and leash training. Cats, on the other hand, do not have this need to please — do not take it personally; they are just more independent. However, cats can still be trained to do things like use the litter box and scratching post.

There is a method of training called clicker training that many claim work well for training both cats and dogs, and it does not require extensive training for the owner. Clicker training uses a small plastic device with a piece of flexible metal that clicks when pressed, and treats to administer as rewards once your pet has associated the good behavior with this sound. The click noise is sharp and consistent so it grabs animals' attention and will not confuse them because of variations, such as the different tones in the human voice. According to Karen Pryor, founder of Karen Pryor Clicker Training, the clicker serves as a more distinct marker signal for your pet, allowing you to shape its behavior in small steps. The idea behind the clicker is positive reinforcement — the animal performs the desired behavior, hears the click, and then receives a treat.

Although you may become discouraged at first, be sure to stay away from ineffective methods of training, such as using punishment instead of positive reinforcement. This includes yelling, spraying the animal with a water bottle, and trying to show the animal what it did wrong. *Problems with punishment methods of training will be discussed in Chapter 7.*

Myth No. 6: Cats and Dogs Require Physical Disciplining

If your cat or dog does something wrong and you do not catch it in the act, there is no way to "show" the animal what it did wrong. Cats and dogs do not have the ability to connect your discipline with their action after the fact because they do not have a good short-term memory. Therefore, dragging your cat over to the shredded chair covering and yelling will only frighten it, not make it understand that scratching furniture is unacceptable. The same goes for dogs — finding an accident on the carpet and shoving your dog's nose into the spot where it had an accident only makes you a bully and will not make the dog understood that relieving itself should be done outside.

More and more, research is showing us that the best discipline for cats and dogs involves redirection and positive reinforcement.

Instead of focusing on the negative actions your new puppy will inevitably perform, praise it heavily when it does something right. Have you heard the saying, "the squeaky wheel gets the grease"? Well, what about the other wheels doing well? What motivation is there to continue good behavior when it is not rewarded or at least acknowledged? You will have happier and better-behaved animals if you are a positive leader rather than a frightening and angry dictator.

This does not mean ignoring unwanted behavior. For cats, make the behavior undesirable. For example, if your cat jumps on counter tops, place a spiky plastic mat where your cat jumps up. These mats are not sharp, just uncomfortable, and will teach your cat not to like that area anymore. You could also place cookie sheets on the counter tops. The sheets will slide and clatter when your cat jumps on them, frightening them and discouraging them from jumping on countertops. For dogs, redirect them as calmly as possible away from whatever it is they are doing wrong, like rooting through the garbage. Bring your dog over to its food bowl or play with it for a minute. The goal is to distract the animal from the bad behavior and reward it for good behavior. Physical reinforcement should only be used with discretion and under certain circumstances. For example, if your pet performs a task well or learns to obey your commands, you can praise it by petting or scratching it in its favorite spots. The key is to use good judgment when disciplining, and never resort to abusing your pet.

Myth No. 7:
A Naughty Puppy Will Grow Out of It

Case Study: Patience is a Virtue

Debbie Margerum, pet owner
Vincennes, Indiana

Debbie Margerum believes that a dog's behavior reflects how its owner trained and raised it. Puppies take cues from their owners to learn what is acceptable, so allowing a puppy to act naughty will make it think it is acceptable. Margerum explains that it takes a lot of patience to guide the puppy. If the household energy is full of anxiety, then the puppy will notice and be anxious as well. Instead, take your time and be patient to teach the puppy to be calmer. When the puppy acts out, it is not always because it has not learned to settle down, but because it wants attention from you.

Puppies are known for being rambunctious, playful, and mischievous, which can seem so adorable when they are small. It is hard to blame them when they misbehave. Some pet owners make the mistake of not training their puppies out of these behaviors while they are young and even end up reinforcing these behaviors that lose their cuteness as quickly as the puppy grows.

When a new puppy barks and jumps up on someone, many people react by cooing and petting the puppy. The puppy sees this as positive reinforcement and is under the impression that it is all right to jump on people. The puppy remembers this positive response as it grows into an adult and will continue to jump up on people. It is important to consider that when puppies grow into bigger dogs, they will not know their own strength. Jumping up on people was fun when they were little, but a bigger dog may knock someone over. You may start to reprimand the dog for it now that it is bigger, but because you waited until it was older, it will take longer for the dog to relearn this new desired behavior. This goes for biting, chewing, and anything else you do not want your dog to do. When a puppy is playing with you it may play-bite, and it will do so as an adult as well if not corrected, which could lead to serious injuries. The dog will not realize that biting hurts, because it thought this behavior was acceptable and will be surprised being reprimanded for biting. You should start your training early to avoid these situations.

Myth No. 8: Spaying or Neutering is Unnecessary or Bad

Many myths about spaying and neutering have appeared mainly as excuses to not have the procedure done, such as myths that the procedure causes weight gain or it is unnecessary because a pet will be strictly indoors and will never mate. The truth is that puppies and kittens are spayed or neutered at an age where they begin to need less food to fulfill their nutritional needs, but many owners continue feeding their pets the same amount or even increase their portion size once the procedure is completed — no wonder cats and dogs seem to gain weight after the procedure. Talk with your veterinarian about your pet's optimum caloric intake, and be sure to allow your pet time and space for exercise to stay in good shape.

As far as only keeping the cat or dog indoors, what owner can truly say he or she knows a cat or dog that will never slip out the front door at an opportune moment? If your cat or dog is left intact, it will have the strong urge to seek out a mate and could try to escape the house to find one. It is better to keep the pet population in control by spaying and neutering your pet. Fixing your pets is also good for their health. Fixed cats and dogs have very little chance of developing cancer associated with the testes, ovaries, and mammary glands. Male cats and dogs will have decreased levels of testosterone, so they will have a sweeter temperament and not spray their scent around the house. Female cats and dogs will also be calmer, as they are not stressed by the desire to mate and will not meow or whine excessively. Also, female cats and dogs will spot bleed during their periods if they are not fixed — something even the most loving owner will probably not want to deal with. Overall, fixed cats and dogs have longer lives due to the decreased risks of potentially fatal conditions and the decreased likelihood of being in dangerous situations.

The last and most common excuse is the expense of spaying or neutering. There are so many low-cost options available across the country that this is no excuse. All local shelters will have this information, as well as the Humane Society of the United States (HSUS) at **www.humanesociety.org** or SPAY/USA at **www .spayusa.org**. If you cannot afford the average one-time cost of $50 to $150, there are organizations listed on these sites that can help you pay for the procedure.

HELP CONTROL THE PET POPULATION

It is likely that spaying and neutering's biggest proponent is Bob Barker, who was the host of the game show The Price is Right for 35 years. Next to the show's popular phrase, "Come on down," most people remember Barker's sign-off advice to "Help control the pet population. Have your pet spayed or neutered." As a vegetarian and an advocate for animals, Barker not only made sure that fur coats were not prizes for the contestants, but also set up a foundation in 1994 called DJ&T Foundation (www.djtfoundation.org) that helps low-cost and free spay/neuter clinics with grants.

Myth No. 9: Happy Cats Purr and Happy Dogs Wag Their Tails

Yes, a happy cat will purr and a happy dog will wag its tail, but happiness is not the only instance in which cats and dogs will show these behaviors. Did you know that cats purr when they are in pain? There is evidence to suggest that the frequency of a cat's purr encourages the healing of broken bones. Also, female cats often purr when in labor, possibly to keep themselves calm and relieve labor pains.

Many people think a dog that wags its tail is a friendly dog, but dogs also wag their tails when they are irritated and possibly ready to bite. The tail is not the only body part that indicates a dog's mood — it is just the most obvious one. These examples show that the context of your cat's or dog's body language and vocalizations matter just as much as the actions and noises themselves.

Myth No. 10: Cats and Dogs Hate to be in Carriers or Crates

Cats and dogs often hate to be put in carriers or crates, but not because they do not like the enclosed space. Cats and dogs actually feel safer in an enclosed space but learn to hate carriers and crates because they were never given any positive experiences around these enclosures.

Do you only bring out your pet's carrier when it is time for a trip to the veterinarian? As you learned in Myth No. 4, cats and dogs are quite intelligent and have learned to associate their crate with a trip to that scary building that smells like hundreds of other animals. Instead of waiting to bring out the carrier, leave it open for your pet to explore on its own. It will probably begin lying inside of its own accord within a short amount of time, especially if you put a comfortable blanket inside.

Crate training is essential for new puppies. A crate keeps your puppy safe while you run errands during the day and when you go to bed at night. Crating also keeps your floors clean so your puppy will not have an accident or tear up the house when you are gone. Some owners see this confinement as cruel, but if a crate is used properly, your puppy will actually enjoy it immensely and seek its shelter willingly. Crates are not meant to hold puppies or adult dogs as punishment or for extended periods of time.

Arriving at the Truth

Now you should have more confidence that you can bring a new puppy in your home, even if you own a cat or two. Remember that even though you may hear horror stories about cats and dogs harming each other, possibly from trusted friends or family members, these are their experiences. Perhaps those people misread the dog's body language and thought it wanted to play with the cat. Maybe their pets were not fixed and thus more aggressive about their territory. If you follow the advice in this book and have healthy, well-adjusted animals, there is no reason they should not be able to learn to coexist in peace and become friends.

You must be patient and committed to this process if you expect positive results. Your cat and new puppy will look to you for guidance, and if you are frustrated or inconsistent with training, you will only confuse them. Remember that with this book, you are training yourself how to interact with your pets just as much as you are training them to interact with each other. If something continually goes wrong, make sure your behavior is correct before you to try blame your pets.

CHAPTER 2

Before You Choose a Puppy

Now that you know it is possible for cats and dogs to get along, you need to examine your cat's personality and consider what breed of dog is best for your family. You also need to look at your family and lifestyle and decide if a puppy that requires significant work and time fits in. Animals have unique personalities and needs. Some pets will have smoother transitions than others, but the best thing you can do is prepare your home and cat for the new arrival as much as possible. This starts with examining your life and finding out how your cat will react to the addition of a canine companion.

Are You Ready for the Puppy?

The decision to bring home a new pet requires you to be committed to the proper time it takes to train a well-behaved pet. You must be present during this house-training phase to be able to correct and to praise your dog every time it eliminates waste. You do not want to have a companion that you cannot trust or that you find to be more work than enjoyment. This is not fair to the puppy or to yourself.

Before you get the puppy, you should read and be familiar with what breeds most fit your personality, the traits of the dogs, and their exercise requirements. Dogs are social creatures that live in packs and do not like being left alone. Dogs will want to be close to you, in the house, and want to interact with their pack members and leader. Do not expect that you can get a dog and just put it in the backyard. Dogs that are chained up or left alone for long periods of time will develop aggressive tendencies, become overly protective, and have a lot of pent up energy that may be difficult to control. If you have not yet adopted your puppy, you may want to ask yourself some questions:

- "Is my family or am I ready to raise a puppy?"

- "Will my lifestyle and schedule allow me proper time and training for my puppy?"

- "What breed of dog best fits me and my family's lifestyle?"

- "How much will it cost me to raise a dog for 10 to 15 years?"

- "Am I ready to alter my schedule and provide a lifetime of care?"

These are pretty big questions, and hopefully you have already considered them and their answers. On the other hand, the reward of this relationship with your new pet is an amazing experience of devotion and love. As Sigmund Freud explained, "Dogs provide affection without ambivalence, the simplicity of a life free from the almost unbearable conflicts of civilization, the beauty of an existence complete in itself."

The physical and mental environment of a puppy's new household should be stable and consistent, and also provide your puppy plenty of time to interact with you. If a household or its members are overly stressed by other commitments, they may have unreasonable expectations of their new puppy. The puppy will need guidance from a human member who is calm, assertive, gives clear instruction, and provides positive, consistent leadership.

Test Your Cat with a Dog

You cannot tell how your cat will react to a dog if it has never seen one before. Not all cats will hiss and run away or attack the puppy; some will allow the dog to approach them. There is only one way to find out ahead of time — bring a friend or family member's dog to your home and conduct a test run. You may think you know your cat's behavior and personality, but these tests will let you see how your cat is likely to react to your new puppy. The personalities of both pets will determine how soon the new puppy can be accepted as a family member, as well as how the cat will

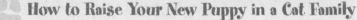

adjust to its presence. It is important to bring this test dog to your home because your cat will act differently in a new environment. You want to see if you can introduce a puppy to your cat, not your cat to a new home. Your cat may guard its territory or may retreat to a safe area of the house. Either way, the point is to know ahead of time how your cat will react.

If you allow your cat to go outside, it may already have had the chance to meet the neighborhood dogs. Your cat will consider parts of the outdoors to be its territory, as well as the inside of your home. Go outside and monitor your cat's behavior. If the dogs outside are restrained by a fence or leash, your cat may be encouraged to be more daring and approach the perimeter. Note how curious or indifferent your cat is to these restrained dogs to get an idea of how it may react to the new puppy.

At this point, you just want to give your cat some exposure to dogs in general. Leading up to the new puppy's homecoming, you can get together with friends who have pets. Invite them over and have them bring their dog along for a pet get-together. Pick friends who know their dog is friendly to cats or are very small and easily restrained. There is no need to introduce a large-breed dog that you know is not cat-friendly. If these friends have visited your home before, your cat has no doubt at least smelled their dog's scent. Your cat needs to practice seeing the owner of the scent and getting to know the new animal.

Place a leash on the dog, even if you know for sure it will be friendly toward the cat. It may be too friendly, and it will help the cat if you are able to quickly pull the dog's wet nose out of its face.

Allow them to approach each other on their own terms. Encourage safe and pleasant actions between the two while standing close enough so your cat knows you are there to protect it. Have treats ready for your cat to reward any good behavior and reinforce the idea that good things happen around the dog. This is a good way to prepare a cat to interact with a dog, since this "test" dog will not stay for long. The animals may play around and smell each other. Next time your friends come over with their dog, the cat will have a replay of the previous visit and will have an easier time greeting the friend. Repeat the same steps and keep everything monitored and casual. See how long it takes for these two to eventually get to know each other. This should give you an idea how your cat might react when you get a dog. The cat will get its first fears of the unknown out of the way and this will lessen the surprise when you introduce it to your new puppy.

A cat's physical reactions

Understanding what your cat is thinking begins with understanding its body language and the various meows and noises it makes. When a cat meows, it can mean various things, including affection, objection, or a greeting. A long meow, sometimes called a yowl, means your cat is distressed for some reason. If you hear your cat making a noise similar to chirping, it may want you or the dog to follow it — mother cats chirp to get a litter of kittens to follow it. When a cat hisses or growls, you know it is angry, upset, or feels annoyed. A hissing cat should be left alone.

You can determine what mood your cat is in through some telltale signs, described here:

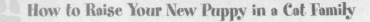
Happy: Sitting, lying, still tail, half-closed eyes, narrowed pupils, ears forward, kneading on soft surfaces, purring

Playful: Alert ears forward; dilated pupils; stalking a toy, person, or animal; pouncing; wrestling; kicking with hind legs

Irritated: Ears twitching back, twitching tail, dilated pupils, growling, putting teeth on instigator, biting, scratching

Nervous: Moving ears to side, dilated pupils, low tail, slinking close to floor, hiding, facing walls

Scared: Ears flat on head; whiskers brought back; arched back; fur standing up; low, erect tail; yowling; hissing; growling

On defense: Crouching, flat ears, whiskers pulled back, tail low between legs, dilated pupils, loud meow, growling, hissing.

Angry/aggressive: Ears pinned back, small pupils, fur on end, low or high tail, staring, growling, yowling

More in-depth details about cat language will be discussed in Chapter 4.

Choose the Best Breed for You

Although we still do not know the exact path dogs took to go from being wild to pets, the dog's strong tie with humans is the result of a relationship that started around 15,000 years ago. A dog considers itself to be a part of a family from its natural instincts as a pack animal. Scientists believe all dogs descend from the wolf, *Canis lupus*. Wolves are well known for traveling in groups with a set hierarchy so much so that humans often call a threatening group of people a "pack of wolves." Dogs, by instinct, are territorial animals. This derives from their tie with wolves, which are extremely territorial. To a domesticated dog, your family is its pack, and your house is its territory.

Throughout history, dogs provided humans with various practical purposes, including hunting, guarding, mountain and water rescue, farming, and herding. For some cultures, such as the Native Americans, dogs played a religious role, helping deceased humans navigate the afterlife; it was the belief in many cultures that dogs served as "escorts" in death. While dogs still fulfill practical purposes today, their place with humans has shifted to emphasize companionship. Many people consider a dog as a best friend or like a child. Some dogs visit the hair salon frequently, wear clothes, and find themselves featured on family Christmas cards. Over time, humans bred specific wolves to accentuate different personality characteristics, abilities, and appearances in different dog types. By researching the original purpose of a dog's breed, you can see if it is likely to befriend your cat or act aggressively.

A dog's individual personality will fully determine its response to a cat, but there are certain behaviors that are strongly associated with certain breeds. While there is no definite answer as to what breeds will get along better with cats, researching these breed characteristics can increase the likelihood of a peaceful home.

The American Kennel Club (AKC) website (**www.akc.org**) lists dog breeds by groups based on alphabetical name, or by different groups, such as sporting, hound, working, terrier, toy, non-sporting, herding, and miscellaneous. There are other breeds beyond this list, but most are not very common. There are resources at the end of this book to guide you to more information about specific dog breeds if you want one that is not listed in this book.

The following are generally accepted as the most family-friendly breeds of dogs that are likely to get along with your cat:

Labrador retrievers

Why family-friendly: While labs exhibit playfulness and curiosity, they are also calm, obedient, and patient with young children throughout the course of their life. They adapt nicely to varying environments, whether you live in the city or out in the country.

What they need: Labs need much more exercise than the typical dog. Additionally, you will need to brush them on a daily basis because they have a greater tendency to shed.

Golden retrievers

Why family-friendly: For an active family, these dogs are ideal because they are always prepared to play. Golden retrievers are cheerful, patient, and easily trained. These beautiful canines have golden coats and a carefree personality.

What they need: Golden retrievers require routine exercise extending beyond daily walks. To avoid tangles and matting in their coats, be sure to brush them regularly.

Boxers

Why family-friendly: Do not be deceived by their muscular, sturdy, guard-dog appearance. Boxers are extremely playful and loyal and create strong, lasting bonds with their family members. Kids will love them, too, for their adventurous nature and curiosity.

What they need: Because boxers frequently need to be outdoors burning off their energy, they match best with owners who have time to play and take them on brisk walks a few times each week. Homes with big yards are ideal, as these dogs love to run around freely. Due to shedding and having short hair, it is recommended to brush them daily.

Collies

Border Collies

Rough Collie

Why family-friendly: With Lassie as a prime example, collies are herding dogs that are instinctively protective of, and patient with, young children. Personality-wise, they are good-spirited, energetic, and well mannered.

What they need: In addition to routine exercise, collies require creative forms of play. Taking your collie to the park and playing a game of fetch or running an obstacle course is a great way to bond. Collies exhibit the most happiness when they are presented with a good challenge. Because they shed, these dogs require regular brushing.

Yorkshire terriers

Why family-friendly: These small dogs get along quite well with children, although it is recommended to hold off on adding a Yorkshire terrier to the family until your children know how to be gentle with the dog. These dogs get along with practically anyone and everything, even cats.

What they need: For families in the city, these little dogs are ideal. The only exercise they really need involves running around the apartment. With their long, silky coat, you will need to shampoo and brush their fur on a regular basis.

Miniature schnauzers

Why family-friendly: Due to their wiry fur coats, these pets are ideal for families who suffer from allergies. Additionally, they do not shed. Personality-wise, miniature schnauzers are highly vocal and rather affectionate. These little dogs can also serve as effective watchdogs.

What they need: Although miniature schnauzers are content relaxing in the house, you need to be aware of their exercise routine. Skipping out on too many walks or play sessions may cause them to gain weight.

Breeds that may take more work

Many breeds described here have specific reasons why they would have trouble getting along with a cat. This does not mean they are bad dogs; they just need the right kind of training to get over this hurdle. If you are a first-time dog owner, these breeds will probably be more than you can handle. You need to get some experience before working with these dogs, as well as have the time to learn about the breed and properly train it.

🐾 **Siberian huskies** have a rough and wild nature. They like spending most of their time getting a workout in the outdoors. They are hard-working dogs and therefore like to play hard too, and could unintentionally hurt a cat.

🐾 **Doberman pinschers** can have a tendency to be aggressive because they are trained to be guard dogs. When they become nervous or scared, they often bite. Train this breed to be friendly by using desensitization techniques or contacting a local trainer for assistance. Also try to teach the dog training commands and you will have a better time introducing it to your cat.

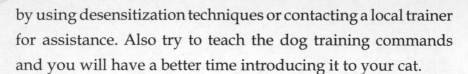 **Irish terriers** are hunting dogs that are often referred to as fearless or daredevils. They are known for their ability to hunt and kill small vermin, and a cat could very easily be thought of as vermin to hunting dogs. These dogs will not have an easy time treating a cat or other dogs as a friend, especially of the same sex.

German shepherds need experienced, available owners. They suffer separation anxiety when left alone for too long. They are also rougher when they want to play and will have a harder time controlling their herding instincts.

Greyhounds are used at the racetrack for a reason — they are the fastest dogs and have a very strong instinct to hunt and kill small game. This breed in particular will be hard to train to not chase your cat like the stuffed rabbit at the track.

While these may be good guidelines for a breed's temperament, you cannot predict the future of the pup's personality without taking it home. You do know that you will be responsible for influencing the puppy's behavior one way or another. Use the knowledge of friends and acquaintances that have dogs. Take advantage of the opportunity to talk with people who have certain breeds of dogs and ask them what their temperaments are like.

Test your puppy's aggressive instincts

There is an easy way to see how aggressive a puppy will likely be toward your cat. Get a stuffed toy that resembles some kind of small animal and throw it past the puppy's line of sight. A dog's instinct to hunt or retrieve is activated by motion: its prey instinct. If the puppy ignores it, it has a low urge to chase prey. If it chases it and brings it back to you, it has a medium urge — a retriever will likely do this, hence its namesake. A high urge where the puppy feels the need to attack and chase prey is evident if the dog not only chases the toy but also grabs it and shakes it in its mouth and growls. If your puppy reacts this way, you need to make sure it understands that the cat is not a toy and does not need to be retrieved or subdued in any way. Through special care and training, these kinds of dogs can learn to look past their natural instincts and obey your command to leave the cat alone.

Mixed Breeds and Designer Dogs

Goldendoodle

The previous groupings and classifications mentioned are called purebred dogs. They have parents that are of the same breed and are therefore easily identifiable by their appearance. Sometimes it may be difficult to tell what breed a dog is simply by looking at it because it is common for a dog to be a mixture of several breeds. These mixed-breed dogs are also referred to as mutts or mongrels. There are many benefits of getting a mixed-breed dog, including the reduced chance of genetic diseases. Remember, purebred dogs are almost always going to be inbred on some scale, which lends to the occurrence of bad genes becoming dominant.

Breeders started a new trend of breeding two purebred dogs to create designer dogs. The resulting puppies display the heterosis effect, or hybrid vigor, meaning their genetic base has broadened. These dogs are often named by mixing the names of the two breeds, similar to how Hollywood couples' names are combined into one. For example, breeding a beagle and a pug would result in a puggle. This breeding allows traits from purebred breeds to come together to create a dog that can display the best characteristics of each breed. Poodles are often chosen as one of the parents because of their soft, non-shedding hair — a trait any dog owner can appreciate.

However, there is no way to tell if that precious Goldendoodle (a golden retriever and poodle mix) or Pekapoo (a Pekingese and poodle mix) is going to lean toward the mother or father's side. Mixed breeding leads to unpredictable turnouts, so it is important that you research both breeds that created the puppy to make sure you like all the possible personality and physical traits. Does the dog come from both a sporting dog and a working dog? A toy breed and a terrier? What if the puppy will have an entirely different temperament from either breed? It will be difficult to pinpoint exactly how a certain mixed-breed dog will do with your cat. Luckily, many owners find that mixed breeds are easy to mold with good training, another attribute that may come from hybrid vigor.

Case Study: Advice from the Author

My Dog Roscoe

My dog Roscoe was a Lhasa apso and poodle mix. Since both of these breeds came from the non-sporting or the "other" category, he really did not have any dominant or specific traits that labeled him as feisty, aggressive, or energetic, and there were no clear signs that he would grow into a big size. Lhasa apsos are known to bark more than other dogs, and my family and I noticed him barking when we had guests. Roscoe only got into barking frenzies when there was someone at the door, just like a Lhasa apso dog would, and he was just acting on that side of his programming. For the most part, his poodle characteristics of being relaxed and companionable with everyone and everything around him, was dominant, and I think this part of his personality reflected how he reacted to other animals.

One Christmas, my family and I decided to take a family portrait that included our pets. Roscoe and my sister's cat, Wiley, were far from picture-perfect. Wiley was a couple years older than 2-year-old Roscoe, so both were still on the young side. Wiley did not know what to think of Roscoe and panicked whenever he came close. We held them for the most part to keep them in the picture, but Wiley tried to run whenever he saw Roscoe. He hissed to indicate he was afraid of the dog, and ended up scratching my sister because she refused to let him go. It was not like she was forcing him to confront the dog, but Wiley still did not appreciate being forced into the same area as this unknown dog.

Roscoe, on the other hand, did not know what to make of Wiley. He wagged his tail when he saw the cat, but he did not want to chase him. My parents knew that it was not in his nature to chase a cat, so they trusted him to walk around on his own. Roscoe just sat still and stared at Wiley to see if he could learn more about him. He kept his distance and only braved a step closer to Wiley when he thought it would be safe. Roscoe did attempt to sniff Wiley's backside once, only to have the cat hiss and jump away. Then Roscoe looked at me as if to say, "What is his deal?"

> Roscoe's first encounter with a cat was bold and brief. The pets were brought together without warning and they quickly had to accept the situation. We monitored their actions so no one got hurt, although my sister received some scratches. If it had not been for the need to get Wiley in the photo, she would have found a better way to let him meet Roscoe without feeling trapped.

How to Choose a Good Breeder

With a large number of puppies in shelters, there are plenty of breeds to choose from when picking out your new puppy. According to the HSUS, 6 million to 8 million cats and dogs enter shelters every year. Every breed of dog also has its own rescue foundation, so you can look them up and see if there are any puppies in your area. If you are set on a certain breed of dog and have not found any at local shelters, you need to know what to look for in a good breeder. There are too many backyard breeders who do not have the best interest of the dog at heart and breed unhealthy pups that do not receive the care they need because the breeders are only trying to make a profit. There are legitimate, wonderful breeders out there who truly care about their puppies, and it is well worth the hunt to purchase a puppy from them. Many people oppose any kind of breeder, but in reality, if we had no breeders, we would have no breeds. Humans created these breeds over hundreds of years, and with their help, these breeds can continue to exist.

Good breeders let you see the mother and father (if he belongs to the breeder), all of the puppies, and the facility. Question any breeder who tries to deny you these basics, as they might be hiding something like a dirty facility. Good breeders want healthy puppies that have the least chance of genetic disease, so ask about the mom and dad to garner the chances that your puppy may have of developing breed-specific conditions such as hip dysplasia. Remember, this person chose to breed these dogs, so if they chose less-than-ideal candidates, they are not doing the breed a favor.

Ask these questions before settling on a breeder

Does this breed have any congenital defects (birth defects)? A good breeder will tell you any and all defects that could happen with their breed.

What do you do to decrease the chance of these defects? A good breeder will test and screen their dogs and will also be certified by organizations that prevent the propagation of such defects.

What are the good and bad points of the mother and father? An honest breeder will give you the good and bad points.

What titles do the mother and father have? A good breeder will have show and working titles.

Where and how are the puppies raised and socialized? It is probably best if the puppies are raised in the house and are used to humans — and other animals.

What is guaranteed with the purchase of a puppy? There should be a contract involved when you purchase from a breeder. Most contracts guarantee a replacement puppy or a refund in the event your puppy ends up with a congenital ailment. On your end of the contract, a good breeder is likely to require you to spay or neuter your pet or return it should you find you can no longer care for it.

Good breeders also want their dogs to be healthy and do not over-breed the adults. Females should only have one or two litters a year and should get a break for a year after that. The puppies should be healthy too, so they should not give you a puppy until it is weaned and at least 8 weeks old — preferably 12 because it is still learning how to behave from its mother and littermates during the 8- to 12-week-old stage.

Because good breeders care about their puppies, they should care about you. They should hound you with questions about your knowledge of the breed, as well as your living conditions and lifestyle. A good breeder wants to find good homes for their puppies, not give them to anyone willing to pay. The puppies should also come with all their paperwork from the vet, as well as any clubs or associations the puppies are registered with. Most good breeders are affiliated with various organizations because they provide them with networking opportunities and show their commitment to continued knowledge of the breed; however, this fact alone does not make a good breeder. You should also have a contract between you and the breeder to ensure you are getting a healthy puppy, to the breeder's knowledge. A contract also shows that the breeder cares about the puppies because he or she will take them back if necessary instead of risking them ending up at a shelter.

Puppies from a good breeder can cost much more than those from a backyard breeder. These puppies can cost anywhere from

$300 to the $1,000 range. When searching for a breeder, you can join breed groups and e-mail lists and use their references and recommendations. Call breeders and ask whom they recommend depending on the breed you are searching for. A good breeder will be nosy and ask you many questions, such as what your living and working situation is like. You will know this is a good breeder because he or she truly cares about finding the puppy a suitable home.

What many people fail to consider is how much time, effort, and expense the breeder puts into these puppies. They also do not realize that a poorly bred dog is more likely to have health problems, which can easily make up the cost of the money saved by purchasing the cheaper puppy. However, do not assume that because a puppy is expensive it means it is well-bred.

Qualities of a Good Breeder

- Has a clean facility
- Lets you see all dogs on the property
- Does not sell puppies under 8 weeks old
- Does not over-breed adult dogs
- Gives you all the puppy's paperwork
- Signs a contract
- Cares about the breed
- Cares about the puppy's new home

Case Study:

What Breed of Dog is Best With Cats?

The following animal lovers, who range from experts to pet owners, give their opinion on the breeds of dogs that get along well with cats.

Shawn Messonnier, D.V.M.
Author of *Natural Health Bible for Dogs & Cats*
Paws & Claws Animal Hospital
Plano, Texas

According to Messonnier, there is no one right answer because behavior is very much an individual thing, and therefore depends on each individual cat's or dog's personality. Messonnier gives this kind of advice all the time on his radio show "Dr. Shawn — The Natural Vet" on Martha Stewart Radio, Sirius 112 and XM 157, Tuesday 7-8 p.m. CST.

Gayle Ballinger, pet owner/head trainer
Pawsitive Steps Dog Training
Seattle, Washington

Breed is pretty much irrelevant; it is not the breed that stands out but rather the dog itself. The individual dog's personality and history, socialization with other animals — especially cats — during the imprint period of puppyhood and development are what will have the greatest effect on whether they can coexist well.

Kim Young, pet owner
San Antonio, Texas

According to Young, any breed of dog will work fine with cats, as long as the owner works on training the dog to learn the cat is not a toy. Young also says breeds that are normally seen to be aggressive are only aggressive because they are trained that way — not because they are naturally aggressive. She has four Dobermans who sleep in bed with one of her cats. Young says that her parents had a pit bull that killed cats, but her brother raised the dog to go after cats. Your dog is going to turn out the way you train it, but the idea is that some can be trained easier than others, according to Young. Even so, there is still the possibility that they will act on their instincts. Young gives the advice that if you are considering a certain type of dog, you must be willing to put in the efforts to properly train it so it is disciplined enough to be trusted on its own. The important thing is that you do not become discouraged and give up on the dog too soon if it is taking you longer than expected.

Laurie Luck, pet owner
Woodbine, Maryland
According to Luck, while any breed or mix of breeds can get along with a cat, there are some breeds that have a reputation for being difficult with cats. People are wrong to assume that a dog is just a dog and will behave the same as every other dog. Luck says dogs bred to chase vermin or herd livestock might have a harder time adjusting to life with a cat. You will find in your research that nearly any kind of dog can overcome its natural instincts with training. Everything depends on the temperament of the dog and its individual personality.

Kurt Salzl, pet owner
Cold Spring, Minnesota
Kurt Salzl learned the hard way: Accidents can happen when a big puppy wants to play. Sasha, Salzl's 45-pound Siberian husky puppy, loved to play with the cats, but she had a hard time controlling herself. One day Sasha decided to play with the cat, Wiley, who was, of course, smaller than she was. Sasha got very rough with Wiley and hurt him so badly that he needed to be put down — Wiley had a broken back. Salzl noted that once Wiley was hurt, Sasha noticed right away and clearly indicated she did not mean to hurt him. Sasha was barking and whimpering and kept licking Wiley and nudging him, hoping he would get up and play. Soon the family members recognized through the dog's behavior that something had happened and investigated the scene. Salzl recalled that Sasha would not leave the cat's side. This example cannot stress enough how important it is to keep the animals supervised until they can be trusted on their own. No one likes accidents, especially if they are fatal.

Nickey Marriott, owner/proprietor
Doggie Haven Bed and Breakfast
Kintnersville, Pennsylvania
According to Marriott, there are certain breeds that may naturally cause harm to a cat. Puppies bred to do certain tasks are not trying to be mean but are reacting to years of selective breeding. Even puppies that are

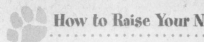
trained to be vicious guard dogs can also be taught not to harm a cat, especially if the dog is brought into a home as a puppy and grows up with a cat.

In the past, Marriott has had a Labrador/shepherd mix, keeshonds, and a Pomeranian, and all have gotten along with her cats. Once her dogs came to respect the family cats, they also learned to respect all cats in general. When it comes to size and breeds, they did not play that much of an important factor. For Marriott, she has had the pleasure of having both big dogs and small dogs and can say they all were able to play nice with the cats.

Preparing both pets for their first meeting will ease the stress of the situation and keep you, the owner, in control. *The next chapter will provide you with tips and guidelines to help you achieve a happy household as quickly as possible.*

CHAPTER 3

Preparing for the Puppy

Dogs are one of the first pets most people consider when thinking about getting a pet, which is one reason why dogs are the most popular pets in the United States, according to the American Pet Products Association (APPA). Before you can prepare your cat for a new puppy, you must be prepared as a responsible owner. The process of researching different breeds of dogs and learning about their differences should also make you realize how different a puppy's needs are compared to that of your adult cat. You are getting more than just a cute bundle of energy when you get a puppy.

Are you ready to handle potty training, late-night barking episodes, and the additional expenses of veterinary care, food, and supplies? Sometimes people forget these aspects of pet care because that puppy is just so darn cute, and they want it so badly. They are focused on all of the joys that come with getting a puppy and want to get them young so they have the longest time together possible. There are other benefits of getting a dog while it is still a puppy besides its appearance and entertaining nature. Puppies are more easily molded because they have not learned any negative behaviors from previous owners. The younger a puppy is adopted and familiarized with people, the more likely it is to be a well-mannered and friendly dog. Remember: No puppy should be taken from its mother before 8 weeks of age. Many states even ban the sale of any puppies younger than 8 weeks.

One drawback to housing a puppy is that it has unlimited and seemingly never-ending amounts of energy, so while its owner may want to stop playing and get some work done, the pup does not. Spending enough quality time with a demanding puppy is important, much like a baby. They are young and dependent and are not ready to be left alone yet. They need constant and immediate attention. If your family has hectic and busy schedules, you should not consider getting a puppy. This is especially true with house-training. If the puppy is left alone for too long while still in the middle of training, it could have accidents around the house while you are out. With a puppy, its dependency also comes with early health issues and concerns. In the beginning, your new puppy will need to take a couple of trips to the vet for check-ups that will include vaccines, deworming, and spaying or neutering.

While this book focuses on adopting or purchasing a puppy, many pet owners choose to get an adult dog. The steps you will take to introduce your adult dog to your cat will be the same; you will just be dealing with a dog that has a more set personality, so any problems will take more work to correct. An advantage to adopting an older dog is that it is possible to skip all of the initial house-training steps that would be involved in raising a new puppy. Another advantage is that older dogs may not be as hyperactive as a puppy. A perfect dog would have a combination of a playful attitude, an easy-going nature, and be house-broken, but that might not be an option. However, just because the dog is older and most likely house-trained does not mean that it is trained in obedience and civility.

One drawback to adopting a dog from a shelter is that it may have a mysterious background. People considering adoption may or may not know the personality and the temperament of the dog simply by looking at it. Before adopting any pet, it is recommended to ask many questions about the pet's history and behavior. The people working at the shelter should have information on each dog available for adoption and be able to answer any question about them. Some of the important questions you should ask include:

- How old is the dog?

- What is the health status of the dog? Does it have a certain diet or any allergies?

- What is the dog's temperament? How does it behave toward strangers and other animals?

- What are its favorite toys/foods?

- What is the dog's background? Where does it come from?

- Has this dog ever interacted with a cat before? If so, how has it treated the cat?

- How does the dog act around other animals?

- Has it shown aggressive tendencies, and if so, what is the trigger?

The downside to skipping the puppy phase is missing out on the fun baby years. Getting new pets that are young, sweet, and innocent are a joy to watch grow under your care. Puppies are fun to play with, and they can bring out youthful energy in anyone who interacts with them. Another downside is that if the dog is well into adulthood or on the brink of seniority, the owners may not get to enjoy as much time with the dog as expected. Of course, people will adopt an older dog for the ability to offer it love and show it the generosity it might never have had. It is never too late to give lonely animals a second chance at life, love, and having a family. No matter what the age, adopting a dog will surely be a worthwhile experience.

Considering Your Schedule

Now that you are considering adding a new member to the family, there are some important changes that will occur when you bring home your new dog.

As you may have already considered, your schedule needs to be altered to accommodate your new family member. If you are alone and are working outside the home, you will need to set aside time during the day to let your puppy outside to relieve itself. This sounds simple, but timing is crucial to allow the puppy to do the right thing and be rewarded. You may want to appeal to your coworkers, friends, family, and neighbors for some help. If you live with your family, engage all members in feeding, playing, and letting the puppy outside. It is important that you explain and carry out the schedule to be consistent and successful during the house-training process.

For example, you let the puppy out of its crate and take it outside at 7 a.m., then let it back inside to feed in the crate. While you are getting ready, the puppy can eat and play with its toys in the crate. At 7:20 a.m., you let the puppy out again to relieve itself and allow some supervised outdoor play, exploration time, and exercise. You put the puppy back in the crate at 7:40 a.m. and leave for work, giving your pet another chance to relieve itself outside immediately before you leave. At 11 a.m., you may leave for an early lunch break or have your neighbor come over to let the puppy out again. You may also feed it again, too. At 2 p.m., perhaps your neighbor can come over again to let the puppy out, and you can walk it again when you get home at 5:15 p.m. As your puppy ages, it will be able to go for longer periods of time in the crate without having to eliminate waste, but it is important for the puppy not to relieve itself in the crate. If family members are home all day with the puppy, you will have an opportunity to involve the whole family in this process.

Supply Checklist

Before you get the pup, you have to get the supplies. Being prepared for the puppy before it arrives at home will help your puppy adjust and will show your cat that change is coming.

Food: Try to purchase the same food your puppy was eating before you adopted it so its stomach does not get upset. If you want to switch to a different brand of food, do so slowly by mixing in the new food a little bit at a time so your puppy can adjust. There are puppy, maintenance, and special diets to meet the needs of many dogs. Puppy and maintenance diets may also be breed-specific to address the special anatomy and nutrition of individual breeds, such as large or toy breeds. Maintenance diets can be followed for adult dogs, or calorie-restricted weight-loss diets can be followed for overweight dogs. There are also several

special diets to address dogs with certain medical conditions such as diabetes or kidney disease. The correct amount to feed your dog depends on the breed, size, activity level, age, temperament, and climate. You can start with the recommendations on the food bag as a starting place, then adjust the amounts if your puppy seems overly hungry or starts getting too chubby.

What you feed your puppy also greatly affects how much and how often it will eliminate waste. Some foods that are high in fat or grains may cause diarrhea, as will excess amounts of canned foods. Choosing high-quality protein sources with few grains or by-products or with added pre- and probiotics will aid the digestibility of the food and the energy your puppy can get through the diet. There are also diets specific for large-breed dogs, and these diets restrict some of the fat to help these puppies not grow too quickly, which may cause bone and growth plate problems. Lower-quality diets will move too quickly through your puppy, causing diarrhea, frequent stools, excess odor, gas, or bloating.

Many high-quality dog foods exist on the market today, and almost all have special formulations for puppies or breed types. There is no contraindication to feeding canned foods, but realize that too much may be too rich for your puppy's digestive tract. It can be mixed with dry food to increase the fiber content and digestibility. For the long term, dry food helps keep a dog's teeth clean, and is better for overall dental health. Many small-breed dogs especially have significant dental disease, often because they have been fed canned food all their life. Canned food may also encourage a more finicky dog. Remember that when you choose a food that agrees with your puppy, you want to try to stick with it. Sudden diet changes or new protein sources can set off a cascade of digestive upset and diarrhea. If you do decide to change diets, mix the new food gradually with the old food over seven to ten days until you are feeding only the new food. This will give your puppy's digestive tract some time to adjust and avoid uncomfortable upsets. Try to avoid foods with grain (corn and wheat) as the first and main ingredient. These foods may cause excessive gas and bloating and may even trigger some food allergies.

Puppies do not have complete development of organ and muscle function at an early age, and this dictates how often they must eat and eliminate waste to maintain proper blood sugar and kidney function.

Do not let your puppy eat your cat's food. Not only will this anger your cat, but your cat's food has more fat in it and can cause your dog to gain weight. If you have issues with your dog eating cat food, you should consider using the meal-feeding method, rather than the free-feeding method where food is present all day for pets. With the meal-feeding method, your pets have limited access to their food at set times each day. *More about feeding methods will be discussed later in this chapter.*

You may also consider buying a large plastic container if you buy your food in bulk to keep it fresh and keep your puppy from helping itself if you accidentally leave the bag out.

Water: Water is something you will already have on hand at your house. Keeping clean, fresh water available at all times is very important to maintain hydration. Water should be offered all day, but during the early phases of house-training (up until 10 weeks or so), you may restrict the water to distinct times. When you offer water to the puppy during the day, let it drink as much as it wants, but until its body matures, you must take the puppy outside within 15 to 20 minutes to allow it to urinate. Do not practice water deprivation to prevent urine accidents; offering your puppy water under your observation allows you to correctly time waste elimination to prevent accidents. You may remove the puppy's water dish one hour before bedtime, and allow your puppy to urinate one more time before you both go to bed to prevent overnight accidents. You are asking for trouble — urinary infections, excessive drinking and vomiting, or dehydration — if you withhold water from your dog. Mixing water in the food will also help maintain good hydration, and many puppies do better if their dry kibble has been pre-moistened to soften it.

Food and water dishes: Your cat and dog need separate dishes. Many owners like auto-feeding food dishes that discharge food as your dog's dish becomes low, but this can encourage obesity in your dog. Purchase a regular dish for food and establish consistent meal times. Food and water dishes come in a variety of sizes, material, colors, and weights. The dishes should be easy to clean and not contain any hazardous materials. Plastic bowls are not recommended because they may leach chemicals into the water; they are lightweight and easy for the puppy to chew; and they may cause sensitive skin reactions from constant contact. Ceramic bowls are heavier and tend not to slide when a dog is eating or drinking. They will eventually begin to accumulate mineral deposits from the water over time and can be more difficult to clean because they are somewhat porous. Stainless steel bowls come in a variety of sizes, are lightweight, and easy to clean and disinfect. Non-tip bowls are especially good for young puppies or overzealous eaters who slide their bowls around. These bowls have a wide base, often with rubber edging, that makes them very difficult for the dog to tip over and spill. Stainless steel buckets for water are designed to hang in the crate, off the ground, and prevents dogs from stepping or playing in their water dish.

Crate: You may use a crate to introduce your cat and puppy, so be sure to have it ready beforehand. Crates are a good way to housebreak your puppy. Some people think that it is cruel to put their dog in a cage, but this is as silly as saying it is cruel to put a baby in a crib. What would be cruel is if you left the baby in the crib and did not feed or change it. The same goes for dogs, and they are comforted in the closed space of the crate as long as they are trained properly. Purchase a crate that has an easy-to-remove tray for any accidents you may have to clean up. The crate should be just big enough for your dog to stand and turn around in comfortably. If you have a puppy that is going to grow into a large dog, you can buy a large crate and install a divider to ensure a snug fit until the puppy is older. If you do not get a crate that is the right size, it will be ineffective for housebreaking your puppy because it can relieve itself in the far corner and not have to deal with it. *How to properly use your puppy's crate will be covered in Chapter 7.*

Blankets: Bedding material for the crate or home should be easy to launder, and special fitting pads can be bought for almost any size crate. Foam bedding is not recommended, especially for a puppy who may get bored or the "diggers" who will quickly destroy the foam and turn it into popcorn. Very expensive foam bedding and orthopedic dog beds can be destroyed in a manner of minutes, even by the most innocent-looking dogs. Expensive bedding may look nice, but you should always be prepared for the fact that your little "angel" may indeed destroy it. Your dog will have no concept or appreciation of the difference between a $5 blanket and a $150 bed. Blankets are to make your puppy more comfortable inside the crate. Old towels work great as well. Only put these in at night until your puppy has better control, otherwise you may have laundry to do every time you place the puppy in the crate. Do not bother purchasing a nice expensive doggy bed until your puppy is house-trained — it will only get ruined.

Collar with ID tag: You may even consider a bell for your puppy or a collar with an ID and rabies tag so your cat knows the puppy's location. If you have a micro-chipped puppy, you still need a collar to attach its leash. Adding a microchip to the back of the neck is a painless and common procedure for both cats and dogs. In Europe, a quarter of pets have microchip implants, whereas only 5 percent of the 130 million pets in the United States have this embedded device. This tiny chip can be scanned with a special gun that displays your pet's unique ID number. The number can then be traced back to your address through the manufacturer's website or phone number. It is still a good idea to attach a physical ID tag to your puppy's collar because not everyone is aware of micro chipping and someone may keep your pet under the impression it is a stray.

When choosing a collar for your dog, you should pick one that fits your dog comfortably and allows at least two fingers width between the neck and collar. The collar should not have excess items hanging from it or things that could fall off easily when the puppy scratches its neck. Characteristics of certain collars might appeal to your particular dog or you as the owner. Nylon collars are easy to clean. Rolled leather collars are good to prevent matting or tangling in long hair. Reflective collars are a nice option if you live in an area with a lot of traffic, or tend to exercise your pet after dark.

Certain collars require a bit of precaution, though. Plastic collars are not recommended because they may stretch and break, and they contain petroleum products and odors that will be very close to the dog's head and face. Choker chains should not be left on the dog because they may catch on objects and strangle your dog if not closely observed. Prong or pinch collars are only recommended in the hands of professional trainers who know how to use them properly for correction of dogs that may be harder to train. These collars are used for correction and must not be left on the dog when he is not in active training times.

Head halters are nice alternatives for dogs that tend to pull excessively, or for elderly or more petite people who may be at risk of being overpowered by their dog. The head halter is not a muzzle. It allows better control of the dog's head, like a halter on the horse. By controlling movement of the head, you control movement of the body without excessive force. The head halter fits over the top of the muzzle and fastens around the back of the head. The leash is attached to a ring underneath the muzzle, and the dog is controlled through the movement of the head.

Some breeds such as bulldogs, Labrador retrievers, and Arctic breeds such as huskies, Samoyeds, and malamutes have tremendous power and strength in pulling ability, and can easily pull humans right off their feet It is important to teach your dog to walk nicely and calmly on a leash and not pull you. This becomes even more important in public areas around other humans and animals, or on wet and icy surfaces. Harnesses encourage most dogs to pull against it with their strength and may make it difficult to control your dog. Harnesses are not recommended for training or to be left on the dog other than when walking.

Leash: You may use your leash for walking your puppy and introducing it to your cat, so be sure to have it ready beforehand. Many owners prefer the leashes that are retractable so they can stop their puppy from running into the road or jumping on a stranger. A short, 4- to 6-foot leash is good for walks outdoors. A longer, 10- to 12-foot leash is good to initially train your puppy indoors and remain in control of his or her actions "at arm's length," while still allowing some freedom to explore the environment. The longer leash is also good for "shy" dogs. It allows them to eliminate waste in their designated area without being under foot, allowing them some privacy at the longer distance. Retractable leashes allow a dog to explore at larger distances, but are difficult to control quickly, may tangle under you or your dog, and are not very strong for hard-pulling or large-breed dogs. Some dogs may also be frightened or intimidated by the sound of the recoil on the leash. The dog may also learn to keep constant tension on the leash while it pulls against it to get farther in front. The goal of leash walking is to have a dog heel by your side and walk with you nicely while maintaining slack in the leash.

Fencing: Outdoor fencing is critical if you live in a busy neighborhood or if your pet has a tendency to wander. Many different fencing supplies are available, ranging from wooden privacy fence to mesh wire. The fence identifies an obvious boundary for waste elimination and protects your pet from escape or danger. Underground fencing is also available. The dog wears a collar that emits a warning or a shock when the dog approaches the fence boundary. Invisible Fence and PetSafe Boundary Control System are two manufacturers of these fencing systems. Regardless of the size of your dog's yard, always keep it clean and pick up fecal matter. This prevents contamination of children who may play there, odor and pest control, and curbs avoidance behavior when an area is soiled.

Carrier: You need a way to get your puppy home safely. Carriers come in many sizes and materials, from small cloth ones to large plastic varieties. The carrier will not only help to calm your puppy for its possible first car ride, it will keep it from distracting you while driving. You will also need it for future trips to the vet and if you ever have to travel with your puppy.

Toys: Your puppy is going to have lots of energy, so make sure you buy some toys to keep it entertained. Purchase toys that will soothe your puppy's growing baby teeth and that are strong enough to handle the abuse, such as Zanies Toughstructable Puppy Teething

Ring or Kong Jawrobics Tuffy dog toys. You will need to replace toys as soon as they begin to deteriorate so your puppy does not choke on broken pieces.

Grooming Supplies: This will vary depending on your puppy's coat type, but you will need some kind of brush to keep its fur smooth and shiny and free from tangles. You will also need shampoo for bath time. Using shampoo made for humans is not a good idea because a dog's skin has a different pH balance, and human shampoos could lead to skin irritation. A dog's skin is also thinner than a human's, and therefore more sensitive to chemicals. Nail clippers are also good to have, such as Four Paws Super Mini Nail Clipper for Pets or Dog 3-in-1 Nail Clipper for medium to large dogs. It will save you time and money to learn how to do this task instead of relying on your vet or a groomer. These can be purchased at Target or online at PetStore.com (**www.petstore.com**).

Poop Scooper/Plastic Bags: No one likes to come across animal feces in his or her yard, park, or neighborhood. There are various methods to cleaning up waste. The simplest method is to use the plastic bags you get from stores. Simply put your hand in the bag and pick up the waste. Turn the bag inside-out so the waste is now inside the bag. Tie the bag and dispose of it. There are also scoops, trowels, and rakes for this purpose, and some come with longer handles in case you are not able to bend over. Figure out what method you want to use to clean up your puppy's waste and buy the appropriate supplies.

Cleaning Supplies: While training your puppy, you should be aware that accidents do happen, so be prepared. Make sure you pick up enzymatic cleaner and paper towels to clean up after your new companion as he or she gets accustomed to the new environment. You should use an enzymatic cleaner like Nature's Miracle or Petastic. Regular carpet cleaners will not remove the scent, and the dog will want to eliminate there again.

You can never have enough paper towels in your arsenal. Always be ready to clean up after your puppy, and you should always keep your puppy's crate and living area clean.

Clicker: If you are interested in clicker training, be sure to pick one up so you can begin using it immediately when you get the puppy home. The Karen Pryor Clicker training store, online at **www.clickertraining.com**, is a great source for picking up the necessary supplies. Additionally, you can find several different clickers online at Nextag (**www.nextag.com**). Do not forget the treats!

Puppy-Proofing

It may have been a while since your cat was a kitten, if you adopted it as a kitten. If you did, you undoubtedly had to do some "kitty-proofing" to your home, and now you must do the same for the new puppy. Puppy-proofing will ensure your puppy stays safe inside the home and out in the yard. It only takes a moment for a puppy to get into trouble, and you may not be able to intervene until it is too late. It is better to prevent dangerous situations altogether.

 Look for any wires or cords that your puppy could reach and chew on. It could easily gnaw through them and possibly get electrocuted or at least receive a decent jolt. Either remove these cords or cover them with an electrical cord cover. There are many options available either at a hardware store or online.

 Get in the habit of putting the toilet seat down. Your puppy will try to drink from the toilets, and the harsh chemicals used to clean them can make it sick.

🐾 Secure your garbage cans, especially small ones that are often in bedrooms and bathrooms. Puppies will dive in, and, depending on what they eat, can develop an intestinal blockage, be poisoned, or even choke.

🐾 Remove any candy dishes from open areas. The candies are usually small and easy to choke on, not to mention the damage the wrapper can do. If the candy is chocolate, it could really make your puppy sick, as chocolate causes vomiting, diarrhea, and possibly abnormal heart rhythms and seizures.

🐾 Do you have stairs in your home? You may need to gate them off until your puppy is a little older, as it may fall down the stairs. The same goes for balconies.

Put Away Poisons

Being so much taller than the puppy, you may not think about common household items that will be on eye level with it. If you take medications, make sure none falls on the floor. It is best to keep the bottles in a cabinet or locked away, as you never know if your puppy may get hold of the entire container and chew through it. Low-level nightstands may be a good place to put your medication so you remember it, but consider the safety of your pets and put it away. Put a note on the nightstand as a reminder instead. Never give your puppy or cat medications without consulting your veterinarian first, regardless of how safe someone might tell you they are. All animals are different, and what was all right for their pet might hurt yours.

Put all household cleaners out of reach or lock up the cabinet under the sink with childproof locks sold in most hardware stores. Cats and dogs are crafty and can learn to open cabinet doors. If you have any pest traps around the house, make sure they are inaccessible to your pets. The poison inside is dangerous to them, as well as the bugs or rodents they are made to kill. When you let your pets outside, consider the chemicals you use on your lawn and in your garden. Does your puppy dig through the fertilizer, or does your cat use the lawn as a litter box? Did you recently treat your lawn for bugs? Your pets clean themselves with their tongues and can easily ingest lawn-care chemicals. Consider nontoxic alternatives, or find a way to keep your pets off of these areas when you spray your lawn.

Eco-Friendly Pet Care

Pets are particularly susceptible to toxic cleaning supplies, so you might want to consider using nontoxic, eco-friendly substitutes for chemical-based products. In 2008, the Environmental Working Group (EWG) collected blood and urine samples from 20 dogs and 37 cats, and the animals displayed traces of 48 out of the 70 industrial chemicals tested. The study showed that more than half of these chemicals had a concentration 2.4 percent to 5 percent higher in pets than in humans. These chemicals are commonly found in food packaging, heavy metals, fire retardants, and stain-proof and stain-resistant coatings. The study suggested that the nature and behavior of domesticated animals puts them at an elevated risk for toxic chemical exposure.

With the contamination of pets comes the risk of families being impacted, as well. The EWG found that the overall health of children may be at risk because of their exposure to these pets. Pets are just as likely to be harmed by these toxins as humans are, leading to harmful consequences for their well-being. As pets age at a faster rate than humans, they are more susceptible to damaging illnesses, such as cancer in dogs and hyperthyroidism in cats.

There are a number of things that can contribute to cat and dog smells around the house. Here are some nontoxic suggestions for eliminating pet odors around the house:

- Change your cat's litter box on a regular basis

- Add baking soda to the litter box to eliminate odors and keep it fresh

- Add coffee grounds to the litter box to serve as a natural deodorizer

- Sprinkle baking soda on pet fur and brush it out to neutralize acidic substances and regulate pH levels

- Clean animal accidents with vinegar to neutralize odors

To keep pets — cats in particular — off windowsills or specific furnishings, spray the area with vinegar. The scent from vinegar also deters cats from scratching upholstery. Be sure to test the spray of vinegar on an area of fabric that will not be seen to be sure it will not cause any staining.

Remove Dangerous Plants

If you have houseplants or let your pets outside, you need to be aware of what plants are toxic to them. While most will not kill them, they surely will not feel good after eating them. We often assume our pets will naturally avoid these plants or only the plants that are harmful to humans are harmful to our pets. This is not the case.

Owners also forget about other plant items around the house, like herbal supplements, herbal teas, or the tobacco in cigarettes. This list of toxic plants is not exhaustive but covers many of the most common plants you will find in stores and from suppliers. These are the common names, rather than Latin names, of the plants. For a complete list of plants that are toxic to your cat and dog, visit the American Society for the Prevention of Cruelty to Animals (ASPCA) website at **www.aspca.org/pet-care/poison-control/plants**.

- Aloe
- Amaryllis*
- Apple (including crabapples)
- Apricot (including Plum, Peach, and Cherry)
- Arrow-Head Vine
- Avocado
- Azalea*
- Baby's Breath
- Begonia
- Branching Ivy (English Ivy*)
- Carnation
- Chamomile
- Christmas Rose
- Chrysanthemum*
- Coleus
- Daffodil
- Dieffenbachia (Dumbcane)
- Fig
- Foxglove
- Gardenia
- Garlic
- Geranium
- Gladiola
- Grapefruit
- Hibiscus
- Holly
- Hyacinth
- Hydrangea
- Iris
- Laurel
- Leek
- Lemon
- Lilies*
- Lily of the Valley
- Lime
- Marijuana*
- Milkweed
- Mistletoe
- Morning Glory
- Mum (Daisy)
- Oleander*
- Orange

🐾 Philodendron   🐾 Schefflera*   🐾 Tulip*

🐾 Poinsettia   🐾 St. John's Wort   🐾 Wisteria

🐾 Pothos*   🐾 Tobacco   🐾 Yew*

🐾 Rhubarb   🐾 Tomato Plant   🐾 Yucca

These plants are considered the most dangerous and should absolutely be removed from your home and yard.

Nontoxic Kitty Litter

You can also consider making your own kitty litter if you are trying to reduce your carbon footprint while keeping your pets happy and healthy. Homemade kitty litter helps you save money and avoid unnecessary chemicals.

1. Shred one entire newspaper into strips and wash it in soapy water using sink detergent

2. Stir newspaper strips and soapy water until it is the consistency of oatmeal

3. Take newspaper mixture and place it in a strainer

4. Rinse with clear, warm tap water

5. Add enough baking soda to the newspaper to soak up any excess moisture

6. Wearing rubber gloves, knead the substance like bread dough, squeezing out excess moisture to dry and break up the substance

7. Break the substance into small pebble-sized pieces

8. Lay it out on a screen to dry, which may take several days

9. When it is dry, put about 2 inches of the paper crumbles in the litter box, scoop out solids daily, and change it once a week

Setting Up a Safe Place For Your Cat

Imagine you woke up one morning to find a random person had moved into your home. You would probably call the police and invest in some new deadbolt locks, not immediately befriend the stranger and make breakfast together. Cats rule the house; you cannot make a cat do something it does not want to do, which is one reason people love these pets. As pets that are not totally "trainable," cats usually walk around their owners' houses like they own them. Your cat is going to feel like your new puppy is a stranger that has invaded its territory, so you need to help your cat understand that a new member of the family is coming. A smooth transition will also make it easier on your puppy to move into a new home.

If your cat does not have a special safe area, now is the time to make one. While you want your cat and dog to become friends, your cat should have a hideaway, such as a cat tree with an enclosed space, so it can be out of sight. A cat tree is a structure designed for cats that can include high ledges, places to hide, a scratching post, toys, and a dangling rope to bat at. Besides being a place to hide, house cats are known for their ability to sleep throughout the entire day, and the hideaway will serve this purpose as well. Cats especially like snuggling up in small, confined spaces. Cat owners are always amazed at the contortionist-like ways cats can fit into a tiny space. This behavior comes from a cat's natural desire to feel warm and protected. Cats usually sleep with one eye open and both ears perked because of their instinct to be alert to dangers. A snug, tight place gives a house cat a place where it can feel safe and protected from danger. A cat tree house can be built to accommodate this. Your cat will feel secure if it has a space that is enclosed on three sides.

Including a scratching post in your cat tree house plans is one way to save your upholstery while still allowing your cat to scratch. A scratching post should be covered in a material that is good for a cat's claws, such as carpeting or upholstery. It should be sturdy enough that a cat can push on it without it falling down, and it should also be tall enough for a cat to fully stretch out while scratching. Wait as long as possible before re-covering a scratching post because a cat's scent is all over its post, and cats prefer clawing shredded materials.

Encourage your cat to use its scratching post by scenting it with catnip and hanging toys off it. Some cat owners simply place catnip leaves around their cat's scratching post to entice their cat to the area. However, if you do not want to end up with leaves strewn around the house, there are several catnip sprays on the market. These nontoxic sprays are made of catnip oils and will draw your cat to toys or posts that you spray. Do not try to make your cat use the scratching post by forcing it to run its claws on it; this will only scare the cat, and it might scratch you.

Besides scratching, you may notice your cat likes to perch on high spots like your countertops — or any high spot it can possibly get to. Remember that a cat's feet paw around in the litter box and walk on the floor, so letting your cat jump on the counter where you prepare meals is unsanitary. Jumping and liking high places is in a cat's natural instincts. In the wild, cats climb trees to hunt, and domesticated cats still have these instincts. Cats are built to jump with strong back muscles and hindquarters, and their claws help them grab onto surfaces when climbing.

A cat's tendency to climb as high as possible also comes from its territorial nature — the higher a cat can get, the better it can see its territory. Height also provides cats a place to retreat when scared or trying to avoid someone or something. You can encourage your cat to use its tree house as a perch by enticing it with some catnip or a toy.

When your cat is not eating, sleeping, or scratching, it is probably playing. Cats can turn virtually anything into a toy. Anything that dangles, rolls, slides, or moves will catch your cat's attention. As natural hunters, a cat's instinct is to stalk and chase its prey; for a house cat, this instinct translates into stalking and chasing toys or moving objects. If you sit on the couch and let your hand dangle off the end, do not be surprised if your cat attacks your hand. This "hunting" is important for your cat because it is how it gets exercise, builds muscle, and stays mentally stimulated. A cat tree house that has a dangling toy will automatically entice your cat and provide hours of entertainment.

Cats value their solitary time, and the puppy may not understand that your cat is just not in the mood to play at the moment. Your cat will be less stressed when it knows it can retreat to its safe area. This safe place for your cat is a good idea during other stressful situations, such as fireworks or a loud storm. If your cat seems disinterested in this new space, try feeding it treats when it does visit the area. It is all about encouraging pleasant experiences for your cat so it will want to continue using its designated space.

Put the majority of your cat's belongings in the cat tree. Before, when it was just you or your family members and your cat, you probably had your cat's things strewn about. Now you must puppy-proof your house, and small cat toys could be a choking hazard to your new dog. Plus, your cat may not like it if all its toys smell like puppy drool. If you think your cat is going to be very frightened of the puppy, designate a room that will be off-limits to the puppy and that houses your cat's litter box and a water dish. Leave some things that are puppy-safe, like a scratching post, outside of this room so that your cat is not quarantined from the family. It is important to provide an area of safe retreat but still encourage your cat to be part of the family. At the very least, move your cat's litter box some place inaccessible to the puppy. Many dogs have the tendency to dig into litter boxes and eat the contents, which is also known as coprophagia. While veterinarians are not positive why dogs do this, it is most likely because it tastes good to them. Cat feces are high in protein, which might be the attractive factor to dogs. Regardless of why they do it, it should not be allowed because the cat litter can seriously harm your puppy's stomach and will surely turn yours just to see the behavior.

Another option is to provide a safe haven in a certain room or area for the puppy, this way your cat can come in — but also hop over the gate when it is finished visiting. Gating off a special area for your new puppy is a good idea anyway, especially if you have a room that has wooden or tile floors that are easier to clean than carpet. A smaller area should also keep your puppy calmer, as it now has fewer smells and objects to explore.

If your cat lives strictly indoors and does not have a collar with your contact information, now is the time to get one. You will be distracted with the new puppy for a while, and you may forget to close the door all the way while running outside to take the pup out. If your cat slips out, the collar gives it a better chance of being returned home safely. Sometimes indoor cats can get away without preventive flea treatment, but now that the puppy will be in and out of the house so often, it is a good idea to start treating your cat with flea medicine before those little pests become a problem. There are many spot treatments available through veterinary offices and pet stores or even online. Some owners do not like using these harsh pesticides on their pets and have found other ways of dealing with fleas. *This will be covered thoroughly in Chapter 8.*

Little by little, incorporate steps to show your cat that there is a new pet coming to the house. Your cat will notice you making special areas for the puppy to eat and sleep and become suspicious as well as curious. You might think at first to keep the cat out of the way while you are doing so, but instead you should have the cat around as much as possible. Your cat will be cognizant of you preparing this new area for the new animal's belongings. Give yourself ample time to prepare before you bring the puppy home so you do not scramble to do it all at the last minute. Making changes in small increments will make the situation less stressful for your cat, as well as prepare any other members of your household for their upcoming responsibilities.

Trimming Your Cat's Claws

First impressions are important for animals, and you do not want your new puppy to be afraid of your cat after it receives a scratched nose for being curious. Trim your cat's claws — front and back. Your cat's back claws are stronger than its front, and it may roll on its back and kick your new puppy. It is not necessary to declaw, or surgically remove your cat's claws, even though this was fairly commonplace in the past. In fact, some believe it is cruel and extremely painful for your cat, as declawing involves removing some bone from the paw. If you feel that trimming your cat's claws

is not enough protection, you can use Soft Paws® (**www.softpaws
.com**), which are vinyl covers that adhere to your cat's claws.

If you have never trimmed your cat's claws, you may find this task difficult. Some prefer to have a vet or professional trim their cat's claws, but it is simple to do once you know how the process works. Before you start the process of trimming, you need to let your cat get used to having its paws touched. Touch them gently when your cat is on your lap a little at a time, and push its claws out by pressing gently on the pads of its toes and the top of its paw. Practice this a few days ahead of the trimming so your cat can get used to this concept. You know your cat is ready to be trimmed when it lets you play with its paws and push out its claws without struggling and fighting.

1. Gather all of the tools to trim your cat's claws, such as the cat clippers, styptic powder, a towel, and treats for the cat. Styptic powder, which can be purchased at PETCO or Walmart, stop the claw from bleeding if you accidentally cut past the quick, which is the area of the claw that contains the blood vessels and nerves; it is darker than the rest of the claw. This is the area you need to be familiar with and locate easily so that you do not cut into it.

2. Set up in a room with the strongest lighting so it is easier to see the quick. Find a comfortable place to sit with your cat in your lap. Your pet will probably struggle, so you will have to use your arm to hold it down or enlist the help of a second person. They can hold and calm your cat while you trim.

3. It may help to wrap your cat in a towel, especially one that is fresh and warm from the dryer. This makes a nice comfortable wrap for your cat, will help put it at ease, and will provide an easier way for you to hold your cat securely

while you are trimming.

4. Slide your fingers under your cat's paw and hold it gently. Place your index finger under a single toe and put your thumb over the same toe. Then squeeze it just enough to make the claw come out. You do not need to apply too much pressure, and it will not hurt your cat. Once this is accomplished, the cat's claw will stay out as long as you hold it, but once you let go, it will go back in.

5. Look for the quick and make sure you do not cut too close to it. You can always trim the nail further if you did not cut it short enough. Cut the claw with one swift clip. Your cat's claws are sensitive, and if you cut slowly the pressure will bother it and it may try to pull away.

6. Continue cutting each of the cat's claws, praising it when it sits still. Do not forget to trim the dewclaw, located on the inner side of the paw.

7. If you accidentally cut too close and end up nipping past the quick, use the styptic powder and apply pressure to the claw right away. In the meantime, your cat is not going to be happy and could bite, squirm, or hiss. Mollify your pet and hold it firmly but gently. Give the cat treats to calm it down. This will reassure it that you are taking care of it. The powder helps to stop the bleeding and heal the wound. If you do not have this type of powder, you can use baby powder or even just cotton to stop the bleeding.

8. With practice, you can do all four paws in one sitting. Get your cat used to this and trim its nails on a regular basis.

9. When you are done, be sure to give your cat a treat for sitting still, being good, and allowing you to finish the job.

Setting Up the Scents

If you can get your cat used to the smell of the new puppy before it arrives, your cat will be less fearful when it sees the pup for the first time. Cats and dogs identify more with their sense of smell than any other sense, so this step can truly help your pets adjust to each other's presence quickly and calmly.

Purchase all your new puppy's supplies and assign them a designated spot. Cats are naturally curious of new items in their territory, so give your cat time to sniff and inspect these items. If you have access to your puppy, gather some of the puppy's belongings and allow it to interact with them so they are marked with its scent. It will let your cat know that these new things belong to another animal as well as familiarize it with the puppy's scent. The dog will also familiarize more with your cat when the cat's scent is on its toys.

If you do not have access to your new pup or have not picked it out yet, introduce your cat to a friend's or relative's dogs. They can help make this easier for you in a lot of ways. Ask to borrow some of their dog's toys, apparel, handkerchiefs, blankets, and leashes. For the time being, mix them with the stuff you have, and place them in areas where the cat will find them. Allow your cat to smell the objects and get familiar with the scent. During this time, the cat will be very curious and not quite sure what to make of it — somehow this foreign smell has found its way into its domain. You may be thinking, "How will it help my cat to get used to another dog's smell instead of my new dog's?" It is important for you to see your cat's initial reaction to a dog's scent, any dog's scent, since it can foreshadow the actual meeting. This will help it realize that there is about to be a change in its environment. Besides, why not teach your cat that all dogs brought into your home can be their friend?

While shopping around for your perfect new puppy, you can check out pet stores that will allow you to handle the pups. There are many pet stores and places that actually encourage people to pick out puppies and give you the chance to meet them — without the glass windows. You can go into special areas where the puppy can roam and play freely at your feet. This will allow you to see a wide variety of breeds, as well as bring home some new smells for your cat. Once you come back home after visiting the puppies, pay attention to your cat and give it the chance to smell your hands and clothes. Make sure your cat does so with the entire family. Do this more than once if you can.

Note: While pet stores are a great place to meet puppies, they may not be the place to get one. Many stores purchase puppies from less-than-reputable breeders, or worse, puppy mills. Puppy mills are places where dogs are bred as often as possible to maximize the owner's profit. They are usually very unsanitary.

Consider adoption from your local animal shelter or from the pet section of Craigslist (www .craigslist.org), a website where anyone can advertise their items, services, jobs, and animals for free. According to the HSUS, 3-4 million cats and dogs are euthanized each year. Even if you are set on a specific breed, you should look at shelters, as 25 percent of dogs in shelters are purebred, and there are many breed-specific rescues throughout the U.S. *There are more resources regarding pet adoption in the back of this book.*

Setting a Schedule and Laying Down Rules

Whether you live alone or have a large family, having a cat accompanied by a new puppy means new responsibilities. Make sure everyone in the house does his or her fair share so the puppy learns to appreciate all members of the family. This will teach the dog to respect everyone instead of favoring certain family members. The first few months can be very demanding, just like having a new baby in the house, while you make sure all of the puppy's needs are met. Your timing is imperative to the success of house-training. Timing should dictate when you feed, when you go outside, and how and when you give your puppy praise. Some simple habits will help keep your puppy on schedule and avoid many mistakes.

This early period of house-training is going to require some alterations to your lifestyle. If you have to work outside the home and leave your puppy in a crate, come home right after work to let the dog relieve itself. This means no more hanging out at happy hour. Your sleep schedule is also going to be altered during this time. No more sleeping in. At 4 months of age, your puppy should be able to hold it through the night without an accident, and your precious sleep will start to be yours again.

You should also give yourself extra time in the morning and the evening for play time and lots of interaction and bonding with your puppy. It is important for your puppy to have lots of exercise and attention from you when you are home so it does not become bored, destructive, or anxious while you are gone. A played-out puppy is a relaxed, calm puppy in the crate. Always take your dog outside upon waking in the morning or after naps, before you leave the house, before going into the crate at night, immediately after removing from the crate, upon returning home, before entering another building, and a final time before you and the dog go to bed. Once your dog is completely house-trained, you can then begin to take your puppy on walks or to the park for exercise.

Sample timeline for an owner who works outside the home, with a puppy younger than 4 months old:

7:15 a.m.	Wake up and let puppy out of crate to go out.
7:25 a.m.	Feed breakfast to puppy.
7:35 a.m.	Potty break. Put puppy back into crate.
8 a.m.	Owner leaves house to go to work.
12 p.m.	Owner comes home for lunch or neighbor lets puppy out of crate.
12:10 p.m.	Neighbor feeds puppy lunch.
12:25 p.m.	Neighbor gives puppy a potty break and puts puppy back into crate.
5:15 p.m.	Owner comes home from work and gives puppy potty break.
6:15 p.m.	Puppy gets another potty break and play time.
7:15 p.m.	Feed puppy dinner.
7:25 p.m.	Puppy gets another potty break.
8:45 p.m.	Potty break and play time.

9:45 p.m.	Final potty break; remove water before bedtime. Put puppy back in crate.

Sample timeline for owner or family member that is home all day, 4- to 6-month-old puppy:

7:30 a.m.	Wake up and take puppy outside to potty.
7:40 a.m.	Bring puppy back inside for supervised play.
8 a.m.	Give puppy food and water.
8:30 a.m.	Take puppy outside for potty break.
8:45 a.m.	Supervised play time with family.
10 a.m.	Puppy goes back into crate if needed while owner runs errands.
12 p.m.	Let puppy out of crate to potty, then feed lunch.
12:30 p.m.	Take puppy outside for potty break.
12:40 p.m.	Supervised play time.
1:30 p.m.	Take outside for potty break. Put back into crate if needed.
4:30 p.m.	Let out of crate and outside for a potty break.
5 p.m.	Feed puppy.
5:30 p.m.	Take puppy outside for potty break.
5:40 p.m.	Supervised play time.
6:15 p.m.	Give puppy water; put it back in crate if needed.
8:15 p.m.	Take puppy outside for potty break.
8:25 p.m.	Supervised play time and family interaction.
9 p.m.	Take puppy outside for potty break.

9:10 p.m.	Put puppy back into crate for short rest.
10:30 p.m.	Take outside for last potty break and back into crate for bedtime.

Sample timeline for owner with puppy older than 6 months of age:

7:30 a.m.	Let dog out of crate for potty.
7:45 a.m.	Feed dog breakfast and get ready to leave for work.
8 a.m.	Put dog in crate. Leave for work.
5:15 p.m.	Arrive home from work and let dog out of crate for potty break.
6:45 p.m.	Let dog outside for potty break and play.
7:30 p.m.	Feed dog dinner.
7:45 p.m.	Let dog outside for potty break.
10:15 p.m.	Let dog outside for final potty break and put back into crate for bedtime.

Sample timeline for older house-trained dog and owner working outside home:

6:45 a.m.	Wake up, take dog outside for potty break.
7:15 a.m.	Feed dog and leave unlimited water.
7:45 a.m.	Take dog outside for potty break before leaving for work. Put back in crate or leave in confined area unattended.
12:15 p.m.	Come home for lunch to let dog out for potty break.
5:30 p.m.	Come from work and let dog out for potty break.

7 p.m.	Feed dog dinner (if eating twice a day).
8 p.m.	Let dog outside for potty break.
10:30 p.m.	Let dog outside again for final potty break before bedtime; place dog in crate if appropriate for night.

Consistency is critical to success, so you should stick to the schedule you develop during this period. A dog must practice a behavior at least 40 times for it to be committed to long-term memory. So, the old adage that "practice makes perfect" stands true. Finding your own key words helps you also establish consistency and repetition in your commands. Consider these words carefully because they should always be on the tip of your tongue, and choose something that you would not be embarrassed to say in a public place where others may hear you. "Do your business," "go potty," and "do your duty" are short, easy, non-offensive, and you will be saying them often. Be creative, but always remember to be consistent.

Do Not Forget About Kitty

The excitement of a new pet can lead to someone forgetting to clean the litter box or forgetting to give the puppy a bath. Creating a job chart is a good organizational tool that ensures your household fully understands the needs of the new puppy and serves as a reminder to continue caring for the cat. Young children will need special motivation to care for pets beyond the fun activities. Even if you do not have children, the chart will help you and your spouse remember what needs to be done every day for the pets. Below is a very simple chart you could write on a dry-erase board mounted to the fridge or on a piece of paper displayed prominently in a common area.

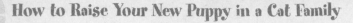
	Monday	Tuesday	Wednesday	Thursday	Friday	Saturday	Sunday
Feeding	Mom	Mom	Dad	Dad	Brother	Brother	Sister
Walking	Dad	Dad	Mom	Mom	Sister	Sister	Brother
Bathing	X	X	X	X	X	Dad	X
Litter Box	Brother	Brother	Sister	Sister	Mom	Mom	Dad

Make your chart work for you. If you want to separate the feeding of the cat and dog into two jobs, do that. If you want to make the chart monthly instead of weekly, go for it. If you have other pets, add them to the chart as well. You can change whatever details you need to accommodate your individual household's needs.

Your household also needs to agree on the rules for the new dog so it does not receive mixed messages. This includes not feeding the dog table scraps, not letting the dog on the leather sofa, and even the wording of training commands. Training should be done as a family for the sake of uniformity as well. Consistency is a key quality of a happy and well-behaved pet household. *This will be discussed further in Chapter 7.*

Budgeting for a Cat and a New Puppy

According to the National Council on Pet Population Study and Policy, the third most common reason for dog abandonment is not having enough money to care for the animal. It is the fourth most common reason for abandoning cats. It is estimated by many organizations such as the ASPCA that almost 4 million pets were euthanized in 2008 in U.S. animal shelters. Many more dogs that do have homes still do not get adequate attention or exercise. They are neglected because their owners failed to recognize the true time, effort, and cost involved in raising a dog. The following figures on cost are not meant to discourage you; rather, they are a way for you to get a ballpark figure on pet-related costs and help you decide whether you can truly afford two pets. If not, ask yourself if you are willing, and able, to cut other items out of your budget to be able to afford two pets.

While there are some situations you cannot foresee, such as an injury that puts you out of work, you can plan a budget for your pets' expenses to give you an idea of how much money you need to set aside. This is a good practice for all of life's expenses, but many people have trouble creating and sticking to a budget as a whole, so they abandon the practice. According to the APPA, pet owners spent $17 billion on their pets in 1996. In 2005, that amount more than doubled to $36.3 billion. Industry analysts believe this increase in spending is due in part to a rise in populations who have a high disposable income. These populations include baby boomers and married couples who have chosen not to have children.

Since you are bringing a creature into your home that will depend on you for survival, you may want to try out your budgeting skills again. First make a list of everything you must purchase for your cat and new puppy. Some items will commonly reoccur, like food, while others may only be one-time expenses.

The costs of owning a cat

This chart represents the average cost of a healthy cat plus any additional, one-time expenses. Initial costs are included for cats as well, even though you already own a cat, just in case you are thinking of getting another. Your costs will vary depending on special situations, such as if your cat requires a special diet or you travel often and must pay for boarding. Also note that the costs of vaccines vary greatly depending on your location, if your cat goes outside, and how long the vaccines last.

The Item	Average Cost Range	Notes
The cat	$50–$1,000 (one time)	Purebred cats cost a small fortune if purchased from a breeder. Adopting a purebred cat from a shelter is relatively inexpensive (starting at $50).
Food	$5–$20 (monthly)	Cheaper cat food has more fillers, which are not as good for your cat as the more expensive food that has more meat.
Food dishes	$1–$65 (one time)	You can get a joined plastic dish from a dollar store or buy a free-flowing water fountain and automatic food dispenser.
Treats	$2–$8 (monthly)	It is better to spend this amount than feed table scraps, no matter how much your cat likes them.
Toys	$0–$5 (monthly)	Cats love boxes, milk caps, and feathers tied with a string. If you are creative, you probably do not have to spend anything.
Collar/Tags	$10–$20 (one time)	The tags often cost more than the collar, usually between $6 and $8.
Litter	$3–$20 (monthly)	Clay litter is cheaper, but clumping litter is much easier to clean.
Litter box	$5–$200 (one time)	Cats prefer the privacy of a hooded litter box (usually around $15), but some owners buy boxes that self-clean or look like nice furniture.
Veterinary visit	$35–$60 (per visit)	This is just the cost to see the vet — not for any shots or blood work.
Vaccines/ Dewormers	$20–$100 (yearly)	Initial vaccines for kittens are much more than annual vaccines for cats. Annual rabies shots can be as low as $15.
Flea medication	$2–$10 (monthly)	This is the cost of topical flea treatment, as it is still the most popular.
Brush	$2–$20	Most people do not have their pet cats professionally groomed, but that is also an option.
Boarding	$12–$30 (per day)	Cats are usually cheaper to board because they are easier to care for, especially if it is only for a few days.

First year total (excluding boarding)	$227–$2,221	This includes all one-time costs, one year's worth of monthly costs, one vet visit, and vaccines.
Monthly totals (excluding boarding)	$16.58–$76.33 (monthly) $198.96–$915.96 (yearly)	This monthly total includes all the monthly expenses, plus the monthly average of one vet visit and vaccines and dewormers.

The costs of owning a dog

With how many products there are available for dogs, you could spend thousands of dollars a year on your puppy with minimal effort. This chart attempts to outline the typical range of what items cost, so it does not include high-end items or extreme vet bills as the result of injury or genetic defect. These items are also the bare minimum, so you may want to purchase more items for your puppy. The size of your dog will also come into play, as a larger dog will obviously eat more food and require a bigger crate and bigger chew toys than smaller dogs.

Extravagant Costs: Pets should have their own space that provides comfort and accommodates their needs. While most pet owners choose to build a simple home, Paris Hilton recently built an extravagant $325,000, 300-square-foot doghouse for her lucky pups. The dog mansion is a two-floor miniature version of the heiress' house and features central air, copper gutters, crown molding, an ornate balcony, leather couches, pink walls, and a black crystal chandelier. Hilton had help adorning the house from popular interior decorator Faye Resnick who decorated the space so beautifully that being "sent to the doghouse" could be considered a good thing.

The Item	Average Cost Range	Notes
The puppy	$50–$2,000 (one time)	Many shelters have adoption fees as low as $50, while purebred dogs from a breeder can cost thousands.
Food	$10–$50 (monthly)	Cheaper food has fillers that are not as good for your dog as the more expensive food, which has more meat.
Food bowls	$2–$65 (one-time)	Most dogs find it easier to eat from dishes that are elevated. Some of the more expensive ones are made of specialty wood or wrought iron.
Treats	$2–$25 (monthly)	There are a wide variety of gourmet specialty treats for dogs.
Leash/Collar/Tags	$15–$50 (one time)	All that matters is that the collar is comfortable and secure.
Toys	$5–$10 (monthly)	Prices for toys depend on how strong your dog's jaw is and how much you spoil it.
Crate	$20–$500 (one time)	If you want a decent crate, you will probably pay around $30-$50, but it also depends on the size of your dog.
Veterinary visit	$35–$60 (per visit)	This is just the cost to see the vet — not for any shots or blood work.
Vaccines/ Dewormers	$80–$200 (yearly)	The first year is the most expensive, and then annual shots are usually around $100.
Fleas/Heartworms	Heartworm: $150 (yearly) Flea: $100–$120 (yearly)	This is the cost for heartworm and flea medications, to be administered every year.
Grooming	$30–$90 (monthly)	If you get your dog professionally groomed, you may not purchase home grooming supplies, but you never know when your dog may really need a bath immediately. Dogs can also go without professional grooming.
Shampoo	$3–$18 (bottle)	Specialty shampoos like organic shampoos or those for dogs with skin conditions are more expensive.

Clippers	$4–$50 (one-time)	There are special clippers that guard against cutting the quick.
Boarding	$12–$55 (per day)	You may never need to board your dog, but at some point someone will likely have to dog-sit, and you should pay that person for the help.
First year total (excluding boarding)	$800–$5,241	This includes all one-time costs, one year of monthly costs, one vet visit, and vaccines.
Monthly totals (excluding boarding)	$59.08–$214.60 (monthly) $708.96-$2,576.04 (yearly)	This monthly total includes all the monthly expenses, plus the average monthly cost of one annual vet visit, vaccines and dewormers, and two bottles of shampoo.

This figure may be a little higher than most people realize they are spending. Remember, these costs are only estimates — your cost may be lower or higher depending on your dog's age, its health, and how many toys, treats, and collars you buy during the year. One trip to an emergency vet clinic or a bout with a bad stomach virus can boost these costs significantly. Chronic allergies, which are fairly common in pets, can represent another added cost for vet visits and prescriptions for the life of your pet. Many owners also supply monthly vitamins.

Inspect Your Puppy

Even if you are told your puppy is healthy and up-to-date on shots, you should inspect it before you bring it home. Puppies can still get sick even if vaccinated because it can take a couple of weeks for the vaccine to reach full preventive power, and the puppy may be exposed to a disease or virus during that time. Also, if the puppy is vaccinated while still drinking its mother's milk, the vaccine is not likely to work because the mother's antibodies will destroy it. Fleas and ticks can also appear at any time, and just because the puppy had none yesterday does not mean one did not hop on today. You do not want your cat to get sick from your new puppy — that is not fun for anyone.

Inspect the puppy's eyes, ears, and nose to see if they are clean. If your puppy came from a kennel setting of any kind, it may acquire an upper respiratory infection, or kennel cough, where the puppy will have a hacking cough. This is hard to avoid when so many dogs are placed together because the viruses that cause kennel cough are very contagious. Many cases are mild, but if the puppy is particularly lethargic, running a fever, or refuses to eat, call your vet immediately. Puppies are not as hardy as adult dogs and might not be able to fight off the cough without antibiotics. Dogs are still contagious for six to 14 weeks even after treatment, so give your puppy lots of time to fully recover if it has kennel cough. It may be possible for your cat to catch the cough from your puppy, so you may have to treat both animals at the same time to ensure your cat does not get kennel cough and then re-infect your puppy.

Setting Up for Your Puppy

Your puppy's setup depends on potty training and how well it gets along with your cat. Assuming your puppy did not come house-trained, you should gate off a part of a room with a tiled floor. Try to choose a room that has quick access to the outdoors so your puppy does not have to go through too many other areas to do its business outside. If you can, make the dog's room one that has a door leading to the outside so the dog's entire domain is in one place. You can include your puppy's crate inside this pen, or you can use it solely for a play area. Believe it or not, your cat will examine how the puppy is trained; it is the best idea to keep the dog and cat domain far apart for this reason. The dog's odors from accidents may have a negative effect on the cat. This could cause the cat to be uncomfortable, as cats are very sensitive to smells. The puppy's training will no doubt be a very foreign concept to the cat.

When it comes to meals, do not free-feed your puppy because it may get confused as to when and how much it can and should eat and where it is acceptable to eliminate. Many cat owners free-feed and will be inclined to do the same with their puppy. You may be worried your dog is not getting enough to eat, but if you follow the serving suggestion on the packaging, it will be fine. The first time you visit your vet, you can double-check the appropriateness of the serving suggestion, as some dogs are more prone to weight gain while others may need extra food. Free-feeding is not a good idea for either of your pets. It encourages obesity, and now that you have two pets, you will not be able to monitor who is eating what. Puppies are attracted to cat food because it has a higher fat content, but they do not need the same amount of fat that cats do. Your cat will also not like the puppy sticking its nose in its food or water dish.

Instead of free-feeding, give your cat a water dish that only it can reach. Your cat is housebroken and thus can have free reign of its water dish because it is not learning proper elimination techniques like your puppy — it already has its designated litter box. If you want to switch your cat from free-feeding to scheduled meals, you may want to wait until it is settled with the puppy's presence so too much change is not occurring at once. Only you can observe your cat's behavior and decide what is best. As for your puppy, set up a feeding schedule that allows you to take it outside about 15 minutes after eating. Only put its food and water dish down for about 15 to 30 minutes, depending on how fast it eats, and then put them away. You can give your puppy more water after play time or after a walk, but until it is potty trained it must wait

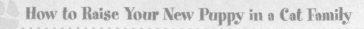
to have freedom of its water dish, because it does not yet realize where it is acceptable to relieve itself.

Case Study:

How Have Other Owners Prepared for Their Puppy?

The following professionals and experienced pet owners share their secrets of preparing their home, family, and cat for the addition of a new puppy.

Myrna Milani, D.V.M.
TippingPoint, Inc. / Bond Consulting Services
Charlestown, New Hampshire
Some pet owners and experts give tips and advice on how they were able to get the dog's scent into their home for the cat to explore. Milani advised to give the pup's breeder cloths to rub on the puppy (if possible) and leave those cloths in the house for the cat to sniff on its own terms for a few weeks before the pup arrives.

Debbie and Eric Margerum, pet owners
Vincennes, Indiana
Get your cat used to the smell of the puppy around the house and also on you and your family members. The Margerum family adopted a puppy from their local Pet Port, which required a waiting period before they could bring the dog home. This allowed the family to visit the puppy whenever they liked — and bring home her scent. They visited the puppy every day, which helped her get accustomed to her new family. When they returned home, they made a point of letting their cats smell their hands and clothes so that the scent would start to become familiar to their cats. They also petted their cats and sat with them so that they would pick up some of the scent on their fur. This activity provided the cat with a first introduction. Smell is very important to animals; it seems like they can understand another animal just by smelling it. These first smell introductions are important to a healthy, happy home when the new pet arrives.

Jeff Marginean, CEO
JEMAR Entertainment Inc.
Host of "My Buddy Butch" radio show
North Canton, Ohio

Jeff Marginean can vouch for getting the new dog's scent as soon as possible and how this can help to introduce it to your cat before the pup comes home. He suggested that once you have chosen a puppy to bring home, whether it is from a pet store, a breeder, or shelter, see if you can borrow cloths that belonged to the puppy to bring home. Introduce these items to the cat. Once the puppy is home for good you can keep up this strategy. It would be a good idea if you could to leave a towel or an old shirt for the dog or pup to sleep on overnight. This idea not only gives the new puppy comfort to sleep in its room for the first time, but also to gather the pup's scent fully. After the pup has slept on the piece of clothing for a night, place it in the area where your cat likes to be or sleep. The cat will come and explore this new smell. The more you do this, the better the chances are of the cat becoming accustomed to the scent of the new puppy. This activity will help to ensure a calm adjustment for the cat.

Najela Cobb, pet owner
Victorville, California

Everyone's preparations will be different, as some will think they need to do more than others. Other people wait until they get the actual pup home to have any actual involvement with their cat. Cobb did not feel she had to do a whole lot to prepare her cat. She found it difficult to work with something that they did not have yet. Cobb described it as kind of like having a new baby. You start bringing in new items and rearranging things to make space and room for the new addition, but you cannot really do much until the new addition arrives. Everyone's life and home situation with pets will be unique, and you will be able to tell what strategies work best for you.

CHAPTER 4

The Language of Cats and Dogs

Cats and dogs may not speak our language, but we can learn to understand theirs. Most of the time, cats and dogs vocalize to get your attention, but we must observe their actions to understand what they are trying to tell us. Body language is very telling, whether your pet is lying on its back, tucking its tail between its legs, or perking up its ears. Owners learn the movements of their pets and can usually decode the meaning of their pet's actions, but this takes time. Cats and dogs are unique, so you can learn more about your pets by watching their everyday actions and reactions. As soon as you can identify your cat's and puppy's behaviors, you will have a much easier time raising the two of them together. This section will help you begin to better understand your new dog's actions as you learn its personality, as well as unveil your cat's often cryptic actions.

Kittens and puppies learn how to behave from their mothers and litter mates. Naturally, because your cat and puppy did not come from the same family, they will behave differently. When they meet for the first time, they will sense the difference in behaviors and body language and thus, there is room for confusion. Your pets will have to learn about each other to send the right signals, and you can help them accomplish this by becoming their mediator.

Cat Communication

Over time, you learn what your cat does to gain your attention and display affection or irritation. Your cat may seek your attention more now with a new puppy in the house, or it may retreat and give you the cold shoulder. Many cat owners see common behavior displayed by their cats and mistake it for something else. When a cat constantly blinks and closes its eyes for a long period of time, many people think the cat is tired and wishes to go to sleep. However, to cats, blinking a lot in the presence of their owner indicates a deep level of love and trust. When they are lying next to a family member and have their eyes shut, they are comfortably enjoying the company of their loved one.

A study of 900 cats and their owners by Peter Borchelt and Victoria Voith with Veterinary Learning Systems found that most people — about 96 percent — talk to their cats. A majority of the owners also felt their cats were able to communicate with them. In fact, about three-quarters of owners believed they could sense their cat's moods. Interestingly, the majority of people talked to their cats as if they were people. Maybe that is because virtually all the owners indicated they felt their cats were a part of their families.

Happiness

Purring is a sign of deep peace and comfort, and usually occurs when you are petting your cat or when you are sitting close together relaxing on the couch. Experts cannot pinpoint the exact mechanics of purring, but they figure a certain vein that passes though the diaphragm causes it. It turns breath into a purring sound from the cat's muscle contractions. This produces a vibration that is both a sound and a feel you can identify when you are close to your cat.

It may seem contradictory, but cats also purr when they are injured or in pain. Listen closely if you are ever around a mother cat giving birth or nursing her young and you will likely hear her purring. Some researchers believe this is because a cat's purr creates a vibration that is between 25 to 150 hertz, which are vibration levels that have been shown to help the healing process of bones and, at the higher vibration levels, tendons and ligaments. Therefore, the mother cat may be providing herself with a kind of general pain relief or even helping her kittens to grow up strong. While this is still being researched, cats do heal faster than dogs and are often used in hospitals to help humans heal faster as well.

Sometimes, a cat will approach its human friends and rub its head along their legs and push its heads into them. This is a form of affection, but it also means a sign of ownership. Cats do this to their owners and family members to show ownership. The cat is demonstrating its possessive nature. With every rub of its head it is saying "I love you; you belong to me." Cats actually have some scent glands on their faces, and by rubbing their faces onto someone they are marking their territory.

Playfulness

Cats play like they hunt. They pursue their toys, ducking down to hide, and then leaping out to pounce. Before pouncing, a cat will wiggle its backside, almost like it is winding up. The difference between play hunting and real hunting is usually how precise the cat's actions are. If a cat is genuinely trying to capture another animal, it will move as quietly and stealthily as possible so as not to warn the prey. During play, a cat will not be as cautious and interact more with the toy rather than stalk it. A cat may also squeak, a quick high-pitched meow, which often signifies playfulness. Normally this means it is happy, but a cat could start to squeak when it is playing with its owner, and other times when it is hungry and is anticipating food.

Attentiveness

Cats are often more alert than we realize. Even while dozing, their ears will flick in the direction of faint sounds. Their ears can also turn in different directions to separate sounds. If a cat seems very alert and focused, it may become aggressive. This can be confusing to owners because the cat just seems very interested in whatever it is looking at.

Aggression

Cats will show aggression with a tense posture, tight mouth, pointed ears, and ramrod straight tail that points downward. It will keep its eyes open very wide to indicate focus, almost as though it is trying to initiate a staring contest. If a cat wants someone or something approaching it to back off, these are the signs to look for. Any tense or rigid body language often indicates aggression. Loud hissing and growling are more often signs of fear than aggression, so a purely aggressive cat is often quiet and confident that it can overcome whatever it sees as a challenge. If a cat is vocalizing while showing aggressive signs, it is fighting out of fear.

Many people are surprised when a cat displays aggression when petted. They think that a cat wants its belly rubbed when it rolls on its back and exposes its stomach. Depending on the cat, it will either let you rub its belly, or it will spring up defensively or may even bite. Lying down on its back in your presence is a gesture of trust. You might be wondering, but if the cat trusts me, why would it retreat when I go to pet it? The belly is a sensitive area, and a cat may be ticklish there. Some cats do not wish to be tickled, but merely want to rest and relax in your presence. Do not ruin this trust by always going to the cat's stomach when it rolls over. Just be content knowing you and your cat can be happy in each other's company.

Fear or Submission

A fearful cat will cower down, flattening its ears and tail against its body in an attempt to look smaller. Its eyes will likely dart back and  forth, looking for a means of escape if necessary. Cowering is also a sign of submission for cats when they have no means of escape and are too terrified to fight back. When a cat is threatened, it will growl and hiss to fend off an intruder. It may also give an occasional high-pitched cry or spit as a more urgent warning. If these vocal cues are ignored, the cat will either run away or swipe at the source of its fear. The best thing you can do for a frightened cat is give it space. Do not make a move to pet it until these vocal cues are not there.

You may find it hard to tell the difference between a frightened cat and an aggressive cat. This is because the two states are often linked. If a cat cannot flee from whatever is frightening it, it will become aggressive and attempt to defend itself. It will arch its back and bush out the fur on its tail. The cat may also turn sideways in an attempt to seem larger, especially with all that puffed out fur. It will hiss and possibly yowl, usually as loud as it can.

The Meaning Behind the Meow

Cats use many variations of the meow to convey their desires and gain attention. Meowing seems to be a domestic cat trait, as no other type of cat seems to speak up like this — the thought of a lion meowing is quite comical. Domestic cats seem to have figured out that humans are not the best at reading their body language and have adapted vocal means of getting our attention. A cat will draw out its meow if it is being ignored or is not heard. If a female cat excessively meows or even moans, she is probably in heat. This can become highly annoying, as it may go on for hours.

Cats may make a chattering sound by clamping their teeth. This occurs mostly when a cat is excited or irritated because it cannot reach its prey. This is a basic instinct that comes from the cat family, so it occurs naturally when a cat sees birds or squirrels outside. Cats could also chatter to show curiosity and interest in discovering or exploring something new, as well as a struggle when they are climbing or pursuing a toy. Cats also make a kind of chirping sound that they use with each other. Cat owners hear this when friendly cats greet each other or when a mother cat and kittens are happy in each other's company. Cats grow to learn to use this as a greeting to their owners when they come home. This is their way to show the happy feelings they have when their owners are with them.

Some cats make hard-to-hear noises but still move their mouths. This may mean their plea is out of human hearing range, so you would have to pay more attention to the body language of a cat that is quiet.

Dog Discourse

Dogs tell us most of what they are feeling through their body positions and movements, while they use their vocals to get our attention. Many times, owners misread these signals because they read the dog's actions in a human context. For instance, an owner sees his dog yawn and assumes he must be tired. This is probably not the case — dogs often yawn when stressed because it brings their heart rate down. The same miscommunications can happen between your cat and new puppy, so it is important to learn how to become their mediator by studying their body language. Pay attention to the position and actions of your dog's eyes, ears, mouth, body, and tail.

Happiness

A happy or content dog will have relaxed, confident body language and perhaps even appear to smile. Its jaw will be relaxed and will likely have its tongue out. A dog may seem content if it is lying down, but if its body is tense or it is cowering, it is not happy. A happy dog will often wag its tail at increasing speeds the more excited it becomes. Most of the time, if your dog is happy, it will want to play or can be easily enticed.

Playfulness

Dogs will often try to invite their owners to play by jumping up and down at their feet or running away only to circle back again. They will wag their tails enthusiastically, unable to contain their excitement, often while looking at you and waiting for you to make a move so they can respond. There are some physical positions dogs go into when they want to play, such as when a dog sits back down on its hind legs and stretches its front legs forward, often referred to as the play bow. This is their way of saying, "All right, your turn! Do something!" Sometimes this position can look threatening if the dog is large or is play growling at the time, but the dog is not being aggressive. Some behaviorists and pet owners say it is not wise to encourage aggression in your puppy, but there is a difference between play and true fighting, and your puppy knows the difference. You must learn how to tell the difference through reading its body language.

Aggression

A dog will do more than growl when displaying true aggression. Its ears will be close to its head, either pulled back or folded forward, and it will bare its teeth. Its tail will be stiff and probably straight away from its body to make it appear as large as possible, and the same goes for its head. The dog's fur may be raised, especially along the spine, although it will be hard to see this on a dog with a long and fluffy coat. An aggressive dog will stare down its target, which is why you should never look a dog in the eye that you are just meeting. It may consider your stare as a challenge and could attack.

When dogs growl, it is usually a form of aggression. This is not always so, and you should take care to know the difference. To identify aggressive behavior, look for a tense posture, bearing of the teeth, and growling. These characteristics could also be signs of a fear that just needs to be subsided. Growling could also come in the sense of playfulness. When you play with a dog, it could growl as a signal that it is being playful and wants you to make a move, such as to chase it or throw something. There is no real audio clue to separate the two growls, so it rests on body language.

Growling plus a laying down position with the paws extended out toward you is an invitation to play.

Fear

A frightened dog will look away from whatever it perceives as a threat. The dog is trying to appear non-threatening and stop you or whatever is scaring it from attacking. A dog will often lower its head as well when it is being reprimanded for misbehavior. Some people take this as their dog ignoring them, but really the dog is afraid or trying to show submissive behavior. A dog may become so frightened that it trembles or even drools. It may also pant or yawn excessively in an attempt to calm itself. Its whole body will be low to the ground with its tail between its legs. A fearful dog can turn into an aggressive dog if it feels it must, so be very cautious and give the dog ample space, or try to remove the object or person causing the fearful reaction.

Submission

A dog may display the same signs for submission as it would for fear, but some will also roll on their backs to show their bellies. The belly area is the most vulnerable part to injury, so this is how the dog shows trust. Reward your dog if it rolls on its back by rubbing its belly and saying "good dog." Submission is not always the same as fear. It is the recognition that someone else is dominant, and the dog is willing to accept that. Most dogs even crave acceptance when they display submissive behavior. If ignored, they may think they are not getting the point across to their owners and escalate their submissive behavior, which could include urinating when greeted. Overall, any tense body language conveys aggression or fear. A calm or happy dog will have a relaxed body and be at ease, with perky ears and a relaxed jaw that may even make it look like it is smiling.

The Meaning Behind the Bark

Dogs use a variety of audio expressions, usually much more than cats. A typical bark could mean a number of things depending on the tone and the volume level. If a dog barks, it is doing so mostly to get your attention. Your dog could bark at you when a stranger is approaching the home, when it needs to go outside, or when it is feeling playful. Dogs have a protective nature over their territory and will bark as a  warning when they feel it is being invaded or threatened. When this is so, they emit a lower-pitched bark at the intruder to indicate the warning. Dogs tend to do this whenever someone enters their territory, such as a mail carrier coming to deliver a package. When a stranger is coming closer, the dog's barks will come more rapidly and will quiet down once they can smell the stranger. A stranger not knowing what is behind the bark could easily be afraid, and take it to mean back off. When dogs bark loudly, it can also mean they are excited.

Higher-pitched barks mean the dog is in need, and this could be the pup's way of telling you it has to go outside, it is hungry, or it wants to play. Your first response to a bark should always be to let the dog outside. If the dog did not need to go out, then you should respond by either feeding or playing afterward. Answering the dog's call to go outside has to be a repetitive routine, especially in the beginning when you are first potty training a puppy.

Another vocal expression that could have various meanings is a whine. Dogs tend to whine when they are in need of something, such as if they are hungry or need to relieve themselves. Watch for signs and clues in the dog's behavior because a whine might also mean pain or injury. A whine could also have the same meaning of a grunt, which is like a greeting to someone. It can be associated with the human sigh to indicate a state of peace and content.

Howling is a vocal expression that originated from wolves. Wolves howl to communicate with other packs, especially if they are further away. Dogs will naturally howl when they hear other dogs howling. Have you ever heard dogs barking and howling at night around your area? Do you notice that all the neighborhood dogs seem to join in, and they are all howling and barking at each other in different intervals? This behavior could be regarded as the dogs getting a little rowdy while participating in the nightly neighborhood bark telephone line.

Can Cats and Dogs Understand Us?

As much as it seems like your new puppy is listening to you when it cocks its head to the side or when your cat meows back after you ask a question, it cannot understand your words the way other humans do. However, cats and dogs can learn the sound of words and associate them with the action they describe. For example, if you say "outside" before opening the door to let your new puppy out to go potty, it will eventually learn that "outside" means that it will go out.

The tone of your voice is also important. Cats and dogs recognize that your high-pitched or cheery voice indicates the situation is good, while your lower or angry voice means the opposite. They cannot understand the complexities of human emotions, so while you may be angry that your pet destroyed a piece of furniture, your tone of voice will only indicate your aggressive behavior and frighten your pet. They will not learn to discontinue the behavior.

First Reactions

The most common problems occur when your cat and puppy misread foreign signals and end up fighting. Puppies are frisky and playful, so when your puppy meets your cat, it may have no qualms about going up to your cat to sniff it. Most cats will be afraid if any animal approaches it so boldly, as cats take this to be an aggressive action. The cat may flee, and most puppies, especially those with higher chase instincts, will see this as an invitation to play. The puppy may not recognize the cat's fear and pet owners may not either, believing the animals are playing. If this is their first meeting, they are probably not playing yet since your cat is not going to be immediately trust the new puppy, even if you have prepared for their meeting. Is your cat hissing and swatting at the puppy with its claws extended? This is not play, and you should restrain your puppy until your cat calms down.

The vocal and body language of your cat and dog will be consistent, but remember, all animals are unique. You know your pets best and may find out your cat or dog has a special way of communicating. Your cat and new puppy will display a combination of sounds and body language when they first meet, and now you will slowly learn to recognize the emotions they are trying to express. You can now act as a mediator between the two animals and safely introduce them to each other.

Case Study

What Are
My Pets Saying?

The following testimonials show that with time you will learn your pet's language and ways to communicate.

Debbie and Eric Margerum, pet owners
Vincennes, Indiana
The Margerums' cats would express tension when they encountered dogs. The cats would arch their backs, signaling the dog to back off. It was the first warning sign before a hiss, which was the final warning sign before swiping. Like dogs, cats use their tails as mood indicators too. Eric Margerum explained that the sharp twitching tail of a cat can indicate a readiness to bring out the claws. Of course, a puppy is not going to understand the cat's warning signs until it figures them out through experience. However, the cat may not stay very long to give off these warning signs to a pup. Any enthusiastic bark of playfulness can send a cat scurrying away before anything else happens. Another behavior cats may not take kindly is having a dog greet them from behind. While both cats and dogs sniff each other's backsides to assess health and identity, cats prefer to give permission to allow this, while dogs take it as a right. It took time for the Margerums' cats to get used to this bold behavior and to become comfortable with the dog. The Margerums said they actually talked to their cats quite a bit before they brought the new puppy home.

Kim Young, pet owner
San Antonio, Texas

Believe it or not, dogs can also have very animated facial expressions. According to pet owner Kim Young, she can tell just by looking at a dog's face if it will be aggressive or not — and this is a big help when deciding which puppy will be all right with a cat. According to Young, you have to watch the eyes when you bring a new dog into a household of cats. Some dogs will have eyes that are wide and alert, which could mean that they are on the hunt for prey. Additionally, Young said you can tell by the way the dog walks toward the cat. If a dog has stiffness in its body, it indicates that it is tense and anticipating an attack.

They had several chats with both of their cats and asked them to please give the new puppy a chance to share the love they had for all of them. This shows how their family focused on talking to their cats in a soothing tone to make sure they did not feel anxious. In the long run, this technique is an effective one that gives all the pets a peaceful feeling around humans.

Teri Dickson, pet owner
Marathon, Florida

Teri Dickson tried to get a good read on her cats, although she recognized that it is pretty hard to read cats' body language. To her, a fluffed up tail is the easiest to recognize. This action means fear, and sharp claws are soon coming out. This demonstration makes it pretty obvious that the cat is uncomfortable. Both the dog and the cat will use its tail to express feelings. While a stiff tail for a cat means fear or curiosity, a stiff tail and crouching behavior from a dog could indicate that the dog is ready for a chase. Dickson advised to read the body language of both animals when they are close to each other.

Babette Gladstein, D.V.M.
New York, New York

Babette Gladstein can tell what a cat's mood is by watching its expression, posture, tail, and ears. She says that ears can say a lot about a cat. A cat is scared when its ears are flat on the head. Open, front-facing ears mean the cat is in an easy-going mood, while ears that are up and attentive denote a self-assured cat. If a cat's ears are angled outward it could signal possible aggression. With dogs, you can tell a lot about how they feel by looking at their tails. Gladstein called this a "tell-tale sign."

If a dog has slow or small wags, this tends to mean the dog is questioning its surroundings. The opposite are large, fast tail wags, which mean a happy or excited dog. Gladstein can also vouch for reading a dog's facial expressions. Dogs tend to have extremely expressive eyes and facial features.

A dog's eyes could portray many feelings. For example, open and wide eyes means the dog is alert or excited in a non-threatening way. Closed and drooping eyes could mean sleepiness, sadness, or submission.

CHAPTER 5

The First Meeting

You have your home, family, and especially your cat ready for the new house mate. You established the official puppy space and set it all up — the bed, toys, and food dishes — and all that is left is to pick up the pup. Surveys by the  APPA have shown that about 26 percent of pet owners have at least one dog and one cat under the same roof.

Do not force the two pets together during initial contact. The cat will need time to adjust to its new furry friend, as it is used to having its territories marked throughout the house. If you have already made preparations, then your cat probably knows that there will be a new animal in the house. Now you must decide on the best method to introduce the puppy to the cat.

Bringing Home the Puppy

You will probably be extremely excited to bring home your new puppy and only want to play with it, but do not forget to introduce the cat. You want to get these two acquainted soon since it takes a lot of time and persistence to train them to behave toward each other. The puppy will smell the cat as soon as it comes into the house and may go looking for it, and you do not want them to find each other on their own. Make sure you know where your cat is before the puppy walks in the door. Have someone go in ahead of you and put your cat in a room where you can shut the door so it does not hide from you and the new puppy.

Take your puppy on a tour of the house, starting with its designated sleeping and eating areas. Allow your puppy time to sniff around its environment and become comfortable. Wait until the puppy is calm to take it to the room to meet your cat. If it is scared, the cat will only scare it more, and if it is overly excited, your cat is likely to become frightened or annoyed. Whatever method you chose to introduce your cat to the new puppy, do not force them together. Forcing your cat to stay with the puppy will teach it to regard the puppy with fear. Your cat will most likely need time to see that the puppy is not an enemy, and your puppy needs time to learn to not to behave like one. This means letting your pets progress at their own rate and not rushing them because of your desire for them to get along. Even if your puppy is small, you should restrain it while it meets your cat. Restraining your cat is not a practical decision since most cats will not tolerate it. Your puppy is more likely to be the one to get excited anyway, so giving it free roam of the room will only excite it more.

Methods of Introduction

Below are three safe methods you can use to introduce your cat and puppy. Consider what you know about your pets before you choose a method. Is your puppy an excitable large breed? Is your cat extremely shy? Catering to your pets' unique personalities will help their introduction go smoothly. Regardless of what method you choose, you should follow these tips:

- 🐾 Keep your voice calm. Shouting will only make a scary situation scarier.

- 🐾 Provide your cat with an out-of-reach spot the puppy cannot reach. This will allow it to feel safer and in control.

- 🐾 Have treats ready for both pets to reward positive actions.

- 🐾 Do not force either pet to interact with the other.

- 🐾 Treat both pets as equals. If you pet one, pet the other.

Separated by a Door

This method provides minimal contact between your cat and puppy. If you were not able to prepare your cat for the puppy's arrival, this is probably the best method to choose. Choose a room with a door that has some space beneath it, and place your cat inside before you bring the puppy inside the house. If none of your doors has clearance, consider buying a gate and blocking off a section of the hallway. Cracking a door may seem like a good idea at first, but your animals may be stronger than you think and push the door open, which could lead to a fight.

If possible, have someone stay in the room with your cat so he or she can observe your cat's actions and be there to soothe it if it becomes upset. Depending on how curious your animals are, they may or may not approach the door. Just remember not to force them to interact. If one of the pets refuses to approach the door, you may have to try a different method of introduction.

Be ready to reward any good behavior if they do interact. It is all right if your cat swats at the puppy under the door as long as its claws are retracted. It is only being curious and trying to interact with the puppy. Depending on how small either animal is, they could fit a great deal of their face or paw under the door. This is actually a good way for the animals to sniff and possibly touch each other without being directly face to face. This will lessen any anxiety either pet has because they do not have to deal with the whole package of the other just yet. The disadvantage of this method of introduction is that the two pets are not able to fully familiarize with each other in their entire shape and form.

Crated Puppy

Puppies enjoy the comfort of a snug crate. Have your puppy's crate waiting when you come home, preferably in a room where you can shut the door so your cat is less likely to run and hide.

However, if your puppy is not used to its crate yet, this may not be the best method to choose. You do not want your puppy to associate the crate with negative experiences, so be sure it is calm and happy in its crate before bringing your cat into the room. Caging your cat is not recommended because it is more likely to feel trapped, even if it normally enjoys its carrier. Your cat may even be offended that it must accommodate for the newcomer.

Encourage your cat to approach the crate by talking softly and showing the puppy affection. Your cat will judge the puppy in part by how you react to it, so if it sees you are having a pleasant experience with it, your cat may be more willing to meet the puppy. The same is true for the puppy — show it that you care for your cat by petting it and giving it treats. This lets your puppy know you want your cat in the house, and it is not a pest the puppy needs to chase away.

When both pets are content, you can allow your puppy to come out of the crate. It would be wise to put a leash on your puppy immediately so it does not spoil the peace by getting too excited, and you may need to temporarily remove your cat from the room to get the leash on your puppy. Seeing the dog on a leash and being separated from the puppy when it is brought out of the crate may instill fear in the cat.

Leashed Puppy

Putting you puppy on a leash will provide your puppy more freedom than a crate, but your puppy may not be leash trained yet. If your puppy is more interested in biting the strange cord you have attached to its collar, this method may not be the best choice. You also do not want it to associate the leash with anything other than going outside, so if your puppy seems frightened, do not try to force the leash onto it.

If your puppy is fine with its leash, put it on before you enter the house. Allow it time to explore the house, and if your puppy is calm and happy, walk it to the room with the cat. You may want to let your pets smell each other under the door before you enter the room. If your cat and puppy still seem curious, open the door so the two can meet face to face. Your cat may flee to the higher ground, but as long as it is still observing the puppy and not displaying aggressive or very fearful behavior, things are going just fine.

The puppy will also learn not to lunge at your cat because of the restriction of the leash. Even if your puppy is only playing, cats do not like the sudden movements of an excited dog. Your puppy must learn to exercise restraint when approaching your cat. When both pets are comfortable with the leashed meeting, you can remove the leash, but still allow your cat that higher ground as a means of escape.

Meeting Multiple Cats

Many cat owners have multiple cats because it is about the same amount of work to care for multiple cats as it is one cat. As long as each gets ample attention, food, a litter box, and you have the money to pay multiple vet bills, they are all set. Bringing home a new puppy is a situation where having multiple cats will increase your responsibilities.

If you have two (or more) cats you should let each cat meet the puppy separately. Presenting multiple cats is too much for the puppy to deal with and too much for you to observe. Focus on the individual needs and personalities of your cats and they will have a better time accepting your puppy. Perhaps one cat is quite bold and would benefit from a leashed meeting, while another is curious but shy and would prefer to have the comfort of a door between it and this new creature.

One benefit of having multiple cats meet your puppy is that the two cats have each other and are not alone to confront the new addition as the only pet in the house. It also means that they are used to having a companion and might accept another friend, even if it is a different animal. They have already gotten used to sharing the home with each other with regards to space and especially with the owners. They know from this experience that the owners will care for both or all of them equally and are not the only ones to receive attention. Having a new dog is just another pet to add to the family, and jealousy will likely be less of an issue. However, one issue that can arise with two or more cats is if they learn how to gang up on the puppy and harass it. If your puppy is especially small, be sure this does not happen, and break up any bullying behavior by making a loud noise to frighten your cats or at least distract them. If you constantly scoop the puppy up and defend it, it may become very needy and never learn to have confidence in itself.

Ready to Roam

Do not assume your pets are ready to roam at the first display of positive reactions. By performing the various methods of meeting you can slowly remove restrictions and see how their reactions change. It may take multiple introductions before your pets are ready to interact on their own. Your puppy needs to be under near-constant supervision until it is house-trained, so even if it does take a while for it to become friends with your cat, it is all right. You can crate your puppy during short time intervals while you are distracted, such as when you are making dinner, or when you need to leave the room, such as to shower.

Continue offering your pets treats when they display good behavior toward each other. Remember to show them equal affection and attention as well. You are their role model and should facilitate their learning and comfort levels. Even if your pets merely tolerate each other, this is fine. They do not need to snuggle together while they sleep to live under the same roof. As long as both pets are not displaying any signs of aggression or stress, you successfully added your puppy as a member of the family.

Even if your cat and puppy get along, special scenarios may arise that could change their new friendship. Is your puppy's instinct to chase high? This could mean it may suddenly chase if your cat darts across its path. While there is no way you can anticipate this, continue to provide your cat with a means of escape, such as higher ground, so it can get away from your puppy if its instincts momentarily take over. Do not close your pets together in the same room without restraint or supervision until they feel fully acquainted and comfortable with each other.

If your cat and puppy do fight, it might be best to let them get it out of their system. This does not apply to true aggressive behavior but the kind of fighting that is a power play, which could arise for a number of reasons but comes down to the animals testing their boundaries. It is similar to a child pestering its parents until they finally break down and punish the child. Just like the child, your pets want to see how much the other will take. However, you should never encourage your animals to fight, even if they are just playing. Their harmless fighting may be amusing, but you are their guardian, and they may mistakenly think they are supposed to fight if you continue to allow that type of behavior.

Another important aspect of allowing your cat and dog to fend for themselves is that they will learn from each other. Maybe your puppy did not mean to invade your cat's personal space, but a quick swipe from the cat teaches it to give the cat more room. It is easier for your pets to learn direct consequences from each other than to try to understand everything through you. Allow your animals to get to know each other on their own once you know they can safely do so. The cat and puppy will get accustomed to each other and may even become good friends, even though they may still become rowdy from time to time. The cat and dog will learn to trust each other but will still send signals to the other one when it is time to back away and stop. Other times your pets will be investigating the great mysteries of the other pet when no one is around or aware. Your cat will take most advantage of the time when it is alone to personally check out the dog and the dog's belongings.

While the puppy is still young, it is likely to want to chase and play with the cat all the time, and while the puppy is still new to the home, the cat will feel some resentment toward the new family member. This is not a conflict that will be solved overnight. During this time, it is crucial to not only spend enough time with the puppy so it is comfortable and adapted to the new home, but you also should spend quality time with the cat to show it is still very much valued.

When can you leave the cat and dog to interact on their own? As you recall from the different meetings, they start out by having the most restrictions, and then little by little the restrictions are taken away until all that is left are the available escape routes. When you use these types of meetings as steps to gradually progress, they will help you get a sense of the comfort levels your cat and puppy develop along the way. You will be able to judge how their progress is coming along whenever you move to the next kind of meeting. Granted, the cat and puppy cannot stay in their cages forever until they are best buddies, the same way the puppy cannot always be on the leash and never go anywhere else. Eventually, you have to use your best judgment to determine when they are ready to handle each other on their own and what action from you is best if you must intervene. Time and consistency will aid you in creating new relationships along with the effort and patience you put in it to ensure a balanced household.

Case Study

How Did Others Have Successful Pet Introductions?

First meetings vary greatly, as you can read from the testimonials below. You will find, too, that your puppy and cat's first meeting is unique.

Myrna Milani, D.V.M.
TippingPoint, Inc. / Bond Consulting Services
Charlestown, New Hampshire

Myrna Milani knows how easy it is to have a frightened cat around a new puppy. She also knows just how much the owners have to do with it. There are plenty of people who allow a cat and dog to fight because they find it amusing. Naïve owners and visitors to a pet home often urge the dog to "get" the cat and otherwise incite the puppy to go after the cat. Because dogs have a much longer history of taking their cues from humans than cats do, the puppy may act on this for the sole purpose of pleasing that person. The more stimulus people feed into the interaction between puppy and cat, the more force both animals will put behind their ways of defense.

Gayle Ballinger, owner/head trainer
Pawsitive Steps Dog Training
Seattle, Washington

If at first you do not know if the pets are fighting or just playing, stay back for a minute and see what happens. Ballinger said the cat is often enjoying some interaction with the dog, but the people are so worried they do not realize the animals are getting to know each other or even playing.

The owners become worried about the puppy hurting the cat, and they end up not allowing enough interaction for them to learn how to act with each other. Ballinger warned not to blame just one for any hostility that occurs.

She stressed that it is not always the hyperactive pup's fault for causing the fight, and the puppy did not always start chasing the cat or irritating it. Sometimes the one that is known to run and hide is eligible to pick a fight. Ballinger frequently sees cats tormenting and teasing a dog; they run off, the dog gives chase, and then the dog is the one in trouble for being naughty when the cat started it all. Sometimes, the cats are being defensive. Most cats will "tell a dog off" and swat its nose if the dog is out of line and bothering the cat.

Teri Dickson, pet owner
Marathon, Florida

Dickson talked about how cats could be both fearful of and aggressive toward the new dog and have no problem showing it. Sometimes right away cats could be hostile, making the puppy shrink back from the hissing and sharp claws. According to Dickson, these cats are actually the ones that teach the puppy manners. A puppy that learns how to behave properly toward a cat from the cat itself is a big plus for the owner who recognizes that the family cat is also doing its part in training the dog. Of course, every cat and every dog is different, and it depends on the personalities of both to see how things turn out. When Dickson introduced her puppy to her cats, she made sure it was well supervised and that no animal was hurt. The goal is for everyone to leave with a good feeling. Through your own body language and tone of voice, you need to be telling your pets how you encourage certain behavior. Calm, quiet behavior around them is the best, as they will pick up on nervousness or excitability, and then this eliminates the need to be too defensive.

Debbie and Eric Margerum, pet owners
Vincennes, Indiana

The Margerum family described how they concentrated on keeping the puppy separated from their cat while they were going through house-training. They kept it separated for the first several weeks until it was properly house-broken.

At the same time, this was allowing the cat the freedom to explore what was taking place without interfering too much. The cat had the opportunity to investigate the puppy's scent and learn to identify it with the new pet. Eric Margerum explained the dog and cat will struggle with boundaries for a while because cats have a strong attachment to territory, and dogs are pack animals that want to be with others. The puppy will want to come into the cat's territory and be included by all the members of the family. It takes time and patience to let them sort things out, and you need to be sure you are establishing where they can and cannot go. Debbie Margerum talked about how the family cats wanted to hide more often and the puppy did not like the idea of being separated from anyone — including the cats.

Nickey Marriott, owner/proprietor
Doggie Haven Bed and Breakfast
Kintnersville, Pennsylvania

Marriott knows that a cat is going to want to take its time to come out and meet the puppy. She explained that as time goes on, the cat will give in to its curiosity and want to come out to see what all the fuss is about. It would want to investigate the puppy in a safe place where the puppy cannot go, and when ready, the cat could come out and give the pup a chance. Their time together will start off short but slowly grow into longer periods of time as they get to know each other.

Sassafras Lowrey, pet owner
New York, New York

Lowrey knows that the outcome of the first meeting depends on the animals as individuals. Most dog experts and owners can agree that there is not one common reaction that will occur when introducing dogs and cats, and it is highly dependent on the individual animal. There are some cats that will be frightened of dogs, and there are others that will be curious. There are some dogs that will try to initiate play with their new feline sibling, others that will attempt to chase, and others that will simply ignore the cat. You might not know how your cat will react, so you need to be prepared for any kind of reaction. Lowrey said that if you are introducing a dog into a cat household, the most important preparation to make for your cat is ensuring it feels safe and that it has spaces to go to get away from the puppy. Your cat might not get a chance to flee to its own room or might not want to, instead wanting to stay in a common area with the family, just wanting to keep away from the dog. Sometimes a cat will just go by the owners when the dog is bothering it or hang out in a cat-only domain. This can be accomplished by dividing your home and creating cat-only rooms or by purchasing or building cat trees. Giving your cat its own space will allow it to interact with the puppy when it is ready.

Najela Cobb, pet owner
Victorville, California
Cobb said that her cat slowly started to allow the dog to approach it. Over a span of time, the cat let the dog get closer, but it still does not hesitate to swipe the dog occasionally when it gets too close. She has also agreed how important it is to allow the animals to duke it out on their own and determine their own personal boundaries and space. Getting back to her cat's and dog's reactions, she has described how they had their own ways to communicate to convey different feelings. Her cat often hisses and arches her back, and in general her dogs usually respond by growling. Normally, the animals will establish their own space themselves according to Cobb's observations. Cobb described how crucial it is to allow the pets to handle things on their own. They may clash for the first few weeks, but they will only stop when they know they can — not when someone tells them so. Cobb knew she had a part to do in ensuring the relationship between the cat and dog would be a good one. She was sure to include the cat with moving the dog in so it could familiarize itself with the dog's scent. Cobb allowed her cat to sniff around the dog's cage while it was outside, for example.

Laurie Luck, certified dog trainer
Woodbine, Maryland
You cannot expect your pets to become best friends overnight. Luck explained it could take a few weeks for your pets to get to know each other, and their relationship will build slowly. For both the cat and the dog, there will be retreats and advances. Each party will be curious and afraid, threatened and excited — just not all at once. As a pet owner, you should expect that general unrest should lead to mutual curiosity and eventual friendship. Both pets will be taking cues and advances off of each other, as well as their family members helping them become comfortable.

Cat owners should practice more caution the older the cat is. Some people wait until their cat is older, or even a senior citizen, before they get a puppy. A common reason for this is because they feel the temperament of the cat will be better and it will not be bothered as much by the puppy than a younger cat would be. There are other times when this pairing would be just the opposite. A laid-back, middle-aged kitty probably will not find the bouncy 12-week-old Labrador puppy at all amusing.

CHAPTER
6

Behavioral
Changes and Issues

Bringing home your new puppy can be a stressful time for you and your pets with all the changes. Your puppy must adjust to a new home and separation from its mother and littermates, and your cat must learn to share your attention and its living space. Cats are particularly resistant to change and may show their dislike of a new situation by acting out. This chapter will cover common ways both of your pets may act out and what you can do to help get them back to their best behavior. It also covers what behaviors are not normal and may be a sign of an illness that requires veterinary care.

Changes in Your Cat's Behavior

Cats do not like change, so any sudden change is in response to a need and not reflective of a cats' true nature. They have very consistent personalities and expect the world to follow suit. This is not how things work, and you can expect your cat to show its disapproval at the dramatic change you have brought to its domain. Cats may in turn do various things you never thought they would do to rebel and express their dissatisfaction toward the change. You can see how a change in routine affects a pet that is so accustomed to something and now has to remold its entire living style around another animal, which is not a very welcoming change. While most of these behaviors will fade away with the appropriate reassurance, some behaviors are signs of illness and need to be addressed by a veterinarian. Your new puppy is going to require much of your attention, but you cannot forget about your feline friend. Observing your cat's behavior throughout the day will give you clues as to what might have caused any changes.

Urinating around the house

There are a number of reasons your cat may suddenly favor going to the bathroom anywhere but its litter box. Start with the easy-to-check, easy-to-fix options if they apply, the first being the cleanliness of the litter box. Has that chore fallen into neglect? You would not enjoy using a filthy bathroom and neither does your cat. This may be its way of telling you to take care of the mess. Or perhaps when you picked up your puppy supplies you saw a brand new kind of litter on sale and thought you would treat your cat. Unfortunately, your cat may see this as an unwanted change and refuse to use this clearly inferior product. If you want to switch litter for a specific reason, such as eco-friendliness or reduced cost, you should gradually mix in the new litter with the old until it is completely replaced.

Your cat urinating around the house could also be a response to the puppy. Male cats may be trying to assert their territory by spraying all that they can. Also, did you remember to move the litter box out of the puppy's reach? If not, your cat may have seen the puppy exploring its box, and now it does not feel safe using it. Moving the litter box to a different place could also cause your cat distress, so moving it a little further everyday to its new location will help make the change more acceptable. This will probably be difficult since you have the puppy now, so hopefully you remembered to move the box beforehand and gave your cat a chance to get used to the new location. You want to avoid changing too much at once — moving the litter box and adding a new puppy at the same time is likely too much change for your cat.

A more serious reason for this behavior could be that your cat is sick. Cats can get urinary tract infections, which are very painful. Since your cat cannot fix an internal issue itself, it tries to solve the problem by changing any possible external causes of the problem — namely, its litter box. Watch to see if your cat cries when in the litter box or seems to be having difficulty going. These are signs that it is time to call the vet. Consider your cat's age as well. Elderly cats often develop behavior issues as a result of their decreased capacity to perform actions the way they used to, such as stepping over a high rim into the litter box. Many age-related

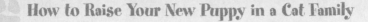

physical changes usually begin to occur anywhere from 7 to 10 years old, and by age 12, most cats are impacted by these differences. You will have to find special ways to accommodate an older cat's needs.

If this problem persists after a visit to the vet and a clean bill of health, be sure you have cleaned the areas where your cat eliminated very thoroughly. Even if the area seems clean to you, your cat may still be able to smell the scent and be drawn back to the area for continued use. After cleaning, cover all areas with some type of protection that your cat will not find so favorable, or use an odor-eliminating spray such as Febreze over the area. Cats do not like the texture on their paws and will not likely tread there. The plastic or vinyl will not absorb the urine, which your cat will also not like because some will surely end up on its paws.

Suddenly silent

Some cats are not very vocal, and this is perfectly fine. Like humans, some cats have reserved personalities. However, if your cat normally is quite vocal and suddenly ceases to be, it is conveying stress or illness. With all the new barking you may not notice that your cat does not meow much anymore, which is why it is essential that you continually keep an eye on your cat so you do not miss subtle changes.

If you see your cat attempting to meow but no sound comes out, it may be ill. The only way to know for sure is to take it to the vet and see if it has an upper respiratory infection or has scratched its throat somehow.

Not eating and weight change

Keep your cat's and puppy's food dishes separated so you can tell how much your cat is eating. Lack of appetite is a sign of many issues such as stress, toothaches, or stomachaches, so it may be hard to figure out what is wrong. Try to entice your cat with especially tasty treats or some wet food on top of its regular dry food. If your cat refuses to eat anything for more than a day, you need to take it to the vet. There are too many possible causes for this issue, and your cat cannot go without food while you try to figure out what is wrong. If your cat becomes overly lethargic and seems very weak, you can spread honey or a nutrient paste on its gums that will bring its sugar levels up, and then call the vet.

If your cat is losing weight, you should first determine how much it is eating. If it is eating more than normal, yet still losing weight, it may have a severe case of intestinal parasites. Your cat is not getting enough nutrients because there are worms living in its intestinal tract that are eating its food. Sometimes you can see pieces of the worms around your cat's anus or in its feces. This will likely require a trip to the vet to receive medication to kill the worms. *This will be discussed further in Chapter 8.*

Scratching and biting

A kitten cannot tell the difference between a second-hand couch and a $5,000 heirloom. Either one will do just fine when it comes to scratching and sharpening their claws. It is a fact — cats love to scratch. In addition to scratching, damage can happen when kittens climb or run over anything made of a fabric surface. This includes your bedspread, curtains, or couch. This is one of the hardest cat habits to break.

If your cat begins scratching on furniture and carpet and it did not used to display this behavior, it is likely trying to get your attention. Your cat may not like sharing your time with the new puppy and knows you always come running when you hear the sound of your belongings being shredded. Scratching also releases your cat's scent through its paws, so your cat may be trying to reclaim its territory from the puppy. Your cat may also be trying to relieve stress, as scratching feels good to cats in general.

Scratching posts can help alleviate destructive scratching. Encourage your cat to play with the scratching post by dragging a toy over it. Another way to deter scratching is the use of a product called Soft Paws®, a soft, lightweight vinyl cap that covers your cat's claws. This prevents your cat from being able to ruin the furniture when it scratches

If you cat is biting you and this is a new behavior, your cat is most likely very upset with you and has changed its viewpoint of you from friend to foe. Biting is an aggressive behavior, so be sure to display nonaggressive behavior in response toward your cat in an attempt to change its mind. Your cat may also need affection. If you have really been ignoring your cat, it may resort to ankle biting to get your attention. If your cat only bites when you touch a specific area, check the spot to see if there are any injuries. Maybe your cat and puppy had a confrontation that escaped your notice.

If your cat has patches of missing fur, it is likely pulling the fur out itself. Observe your cat and see when it grooms itself. Does it suddenly stop to bite the spot and aggressively lick the area? Something is likely irritating your cat's skin, such as a parasite or an allergy. Your cat may also be in pain and is trying to heal itself. If it just over-grooms itself, it is likely stressed, as grooming is a calming action for cats.

Climbing

Have you noticed your cat favoring elevated areas since you brought the puppy home? Cats express dominance by towering over other animals, so gazing down at the puppy from the top of the china cabinet makes your cat feel powerful. Cats also enjoy surveying as much of their territory at one time as possible, so your cat may just be entertaining itself. If you do not want your cat climbing on certain pieces of furniture because you have fragile items you are worried about your cat knocking over, you can cover these areas with a texture your cat will not like, such as bubble wrap, until your cat learns not to jump to these areas. It is important that you do not take away all the possible climbing spots for your cat so there will still be places to escape to and hide from the puppy. To keep your cat off of specific furnishings, spray the area with vinegar. Additionally, the scent from vinegar also deters cats from scratching the upholstery. Be sure to test the spray of vinegar on an area of fabric that will not be seen to be sure it will not cause any staining.

Hiding

Your cat may stay hidden for days or even weeks if it is particularly frightened of the puppy. It might think that there are no safe times and stay hidden to avoid bumping into the dog and being frightened all over again. It is going to stress out not knowing when it can come out. Frightened cats can turn their fear into aggression, especially when they feel like even their hiding place has become disturbed and unsafe. This can be when the puppy has found the cat's hiding place and will not leave it alone or even when the cat's owners push the cat to come out. The best thing you can do is encourage your cat to come out by offering treats, and if it does not want to leave its spot, just let it stay there. More than likely, it is not hurting anything for your cat to stay hidden. Forcing your cat to come out will only stress it out more. Make sure your cat is fulfilling its needs during this period of hiding. Sick cats often go into hiding because they feel vulnerable, so make sure your cat is just shy and not sick by checking up on it every now and then.

Your Cat's Troubled Emotions

There is uncertainty regarding whether cats have true emotions, as some scientists believe cats only use humans for food and shelter, yet most owners think they are sensitive and have an array of emotions. Certain basic emotions, often called primary emotions, like happiness and fear are triggered in all species of animals through the release of hormones in the brain. All creatures that hope to survive in nature must be able to distinguish good things from bad things or the survival rate of that creature would plummet. In addition to these basic emotions, humans have developed a complex array of additional emotions, often called secondary or tertiary emotions, that are based on our social structure and interactions with other humans, such as shame and guilt.

Some people criticize those who compare their cat's emotions to human emotions because we are not the same species, and many humans also think we are the superior species. Emotions are our mental response to our environment. Cats display plenty of behavior that demonstrates their emotions, but humans must remember that no matter how much we love our pets, they are not human and do not think like humans. Owners must learn to think like a cat to understand why cats act the way they do.

Jealousy

Jealousy is considered a more complex human emotion, but cats display behavior that seems like jealousy to their owners. For example, if your puppy decides to lay down in your cat's favorite spot by the sun-lit sliding glass door, your cat may react by becoming aggressive or by retreating to an unusual area of the house. Surely your cat is jealous of the puppy, right? In reality, your cat probably does not think of the puppy as having qualities or items that it wants, which is the human definition of jealousy. Cats are territorial, and if your cat thinks it is strong enough, it will fight for the territory, and if not, it will retreat. The puppy has caused a change in your cat's life, so naturally your cat is miffed.

The same idea applies to your cat being jealous of the attention the new puppy is receiving. It is not that the cat wants what the puppy has; it is just used to a certain amount of attention from you, and if you change that amount, your cat will not be pleased. Cats are comforted by the routines in their lives and look forward to events like set meal times and the sound of your alarm clock because it gives them a sense of security — they know what's going to take place. When a change interrupts the routine that the cat expects, the cat is disturbed because it does not know what

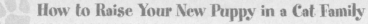

else could change. When this change goes on and keeps the cat from returning to normalcy, it can cause the cat to have high stress levels. The best thing you can do is minimize the changes to your cat's routine and bring the changes in as slowly as you can.

Spite

When your cat tears up your favorite shirt you left out for work the next morning or knocks over a glass of water and reduces your newspaper to mush, you may feel like it is being purposely spiteful. It knows you brought that awful ball of barking fur into its house, and it wants revenge. Again, there is no definite proof that cats can act out in this manner on a conscious level, but many cat owners agree that some cats do get mad and will take it out on whatever caused them to be mad. Consider the situation like your cat would. Maybe your shirt just felt really good to knead, and the water in that glass is as entertaining as a toy when it runs in rivulets down the cracks of the table. Your cat will always behave in predictable ways; you just need to recognize its patterns.

Depression

Almost conversely, cats display depression much like humans do. They can become disinterested in everyday activities and withdrawn from their lives. They may stop playing or meowing, or lose their appetites. Cats become depressed when they lose a family member, and even seem to comprehend the ultimate meaning of death. It is best to leave your cat home when going to a funeral. If shown the body of a deceased owner or fellow feline, the cat can smell the difference from when it was alive and sense the difference in body temperature. Cats will usually stop looking for the missing companion if shown the body — however, it is unlikely you will be able to bring your cat to a funeral. Your cat may also become depressed if it has extreme difficulty adjusting to the puppy because the stress turns to depression. Prolonged depression can overcome a cat's spirits, so owners must monitor their cat's behaviors to ensure they are eating and fulfilling their basic needs.

Alleviating Your Cat's Stress

Whether your cat shows physical or emotional signs of stress, as a caring owner you will want to do all that you can to help your cat feel calmer and get back into a happy routine. It will be difficult for your cat to accept changes such as this all at once. It is crucial to allow your cat the space it needs for comfort as well as play and exercise. Your cat will feel stressed out when it seems like its personal space is being invaded. Your cat's room may be its place of haven, but take a look at it as well. Is it too cramped even in there? Space can be physical and emotional. Not only does you cat need a physical living area, but you also need to allow your cat to be left alone to hide until it feels comfortable coming out. At the same time, cats need loving attention from their owners while they are getting to learn to have companionship with the new puppy. Spend some quality time with your cat to remind it that you still care for it and to help take its mind off the canine intruder. Hold and pet your cat often, and especially when the puppy is in sight so the cat realizes it is still loved and holds a place in your heart, despite the puppy's presence. This will also provide comfort for your cat and give it time to relieve its stress and come out of hiding.

Changing your cat's diet may be something to consider for a stressed out cat. You can supply your cat with healthier options in meals as well as treats, and anything recommended from a vet that will let your cat relax. Some examples of healthy cat food include Life's Abundance Gourmet Cat Treats for Healthy Skin & Coat, Whiskas Temptations Cat Treats, and Zuke's Natural Purrz Healthy, Moist Cat Treats. Along with good dieting and healing supplements, your cat needs good exercise. Keep your cat happy by keeping it busy, and continue its usual play activity with its favorite toys. Get some new toys and new climbing areas for your cat, such as posts it can climb on, scratch, and sit atop and watch the happenings of the room. Exercise is a good stress reliever for humans, and it works with pets as well. Together with exercise and good nutrition, you can prevent your cat from becoming obese, as sometimes overeating is the result of an upset and stressed out cat.

There are many things you can do during this time to be sure you do not lose your cat's love and trust during the puppy's incorporation into your family. Begin by seeing a vet to get a professional's insight if your cat does have a problem. You can provide details of the changes in your cat's behavior to help your vet better analyze your cat's actions and provide the best remedies. At home, it is important to keep up the same things you have always had with your cat to maintain the same familiarity.

Continuing habits with your cat while raising the new puppy is a challenge, but you will find that it becomes easier once the puppy becomes accustomed to the home. Soon your cat will go about its life like normal. Your goal is to make sure your cat is occupied enough by its daily life and the pleasures associated with it: toys, food, leisure, relaxation, and affection and attention by you and your other family members. This is so your cat does not feel its own security threatened and instead learns to see the puppy as a new friend that it can enjoy its pleasures with.

Normal Puppy Behavior

Raising a puppy is often compared to raising a child in a very short amount of time. This causes many owners to worry and fret over everything regarding their new pet, which is not necessary once the normal behaviors of puppies are understood, and the signs of sickness and stress are recognizable. Your puppy is going to pick up on the vibes you send out, so if you are worried or upset all the time, your puppy is likely to be worried and upset as well. Educate yourself about the needs of your puppy so you can present confidence and control that your puppy can learn and be comforted by.

Dependency

Dogs retain many of the behaviors of their ancestors, even though they are living in a much more modern world with humans. The live in small social groups, follow a leader, and show territorial protection. They have a hierarchical social system that is relatively stable, and this structure helps to prevent aggressive confrontations. Dogs use complex body language to exhibit dominant and submissive posture to maintain their social structure. In the domestic life of dogs living with their pack of humans, it is important that humans maintain the leadership role in the household.

Unlike your cat, your new puppy is not going to want to be alone. It will likely have difficulty sleeping through the first few nights in its new home with you. Expect its behavior to be similar to a baby's behavior. It will bark and cry for attention and will not find it easy to go to sleep. The puppy is just scared to be in a new place. It is a good sign that the pup barks for you and responds to you caring for it since it already identified you as its caretaker and trusts you. What you need to do is provide your puppy some comfort in its bed.

Case Study: Advice from the Author

My Dog Roscoe

When my dog Roscoe had his first night alone in his bed, he was not happy about it. He would bark and keep trying to come into someone's room to sleep for the night, and my family would insist he sleep in his own bed. He had both a bed and a cage and it was decided for him to spend nights in the cage for safety confinement. The goal was to cage-train him not only for bathroom reasons, but also to have him get used to his cage and the fact that it was his designated place to sleep, but Roscoe had other ideas. As a Lhasa Apso and poodle mix, he was a small enough pup to squeeze under the bars in the cage and roam around until he could find somewhere better to sleep. The next morning we found him snug up and fast asleep on my pillow on the couch. He smelled my scent on there and thought to himself that if he could not be with his owners while sleeping, then they could be with him. This proves how strong scent and identifying familiarity mean to pets. Like many dogs, Roscoe became afraid and needed a familiar comfort to feel safe and secure.

Some people allow their puppy to sleep in bed with them, and while this may solve the immediate problem of a needy puppy, it will create a slew of issues you may not consider until it is too late. First, your puppy is going to bring hair, dirt, drool, and whatever else it picked up throughout the day into bed with you. It is one thing to love your puppy, but it is another thing to smell like your puppy. Also, do you really want to fight your puppy for space in bed? If your puppy is a large breed, it could easily take up most of the space on your bed, forcing you to struggle every night to get enough room. Do not fool yourself into thinking the puppy will only sleep with you for a few nights while it adjusts, then move without hassle to its crate or bed. It will be just as upset as it was before, if not worse, because it knows it can get away with sleeping in your bed. Your puppy needs to learn to find security within itself so it does not suffer from separation anxiety every time you leave the house and it cannot come with you. Separation anxiety can cause your puppy to act out in destructive ways, such as chewing up shoes or suddenly forgetting its housebreaking lessons.

Are you training your puppy to stay off of the furniture but letting it sleep in bed with you? That is going to confuse your puppy, which will always want to join you on whatever piece of furniture you are using. Consistency is key, so if you do not want your puppy on the sofa, the bed should be off limits as well. Instead, your puppy needs places like its crate and bed that belong solely to it. This teaches the puppy to respect your furniture by leaving

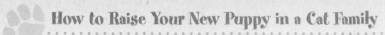

it alone and to value its furniture as safe areas where no one else will bother it.

Do not forget about both of your pets — do they normally sleep with you, even if only for a couple of hours a night? You can guess by now that your cat will not enjoy sharing the bed with the puppy, and you may be woken up at 3 a.m. to deal with a dispute over who gets to sleep against your side. If your cat did not sleep with you in the past, it will still see that the puppy is allowed to and wonder why the puppy can share your territory, but it cannot. You may want the puppy to sleep in its crate on the floor of your room if your cat objects to it sharing the bed. This way, both animals can enjoy the comfort of sleeping in your presence and in your room.

You and your new puppy may not want to separate for the night, but it is for the best in the long run. You can incorporate your smell for the puppy in its room or on its bed. You want your puppy to sleep soundly knowing that you are nearby, and you protect it. You can put an article of clothing that belongs to each family member in the puppy's bed. Once your puppy learns your smells and becomes comforted by them, he or she will start to familiarize with the home and learn to adjust quickly.

Barking and communication

Dogs use a variety of visual, olfactory, and vocal cues to communicate with each other. These cues help to transmit a variety of messages to other and from other dogs. These cues help the dog to determine if a message is friendly or threatening. Vocalization can communicate caution with a growl, or alerting with a bark. Dogs use their body language to communicate visual cues to other dogs. A dog may maximize its size to appear more threatening and protective, as a dog that curls up or rolls on its back indicates submission. Scent is a highly evolved sense in dogs that tells them a great deal about their environment and each other. Is it male or female? Is it receptive to breeding? Who was here last? What animals or humans have passed through here? Is it friend or foe?

It is normal for your puppy to bark since it is the way it gains your attention. Any external stimuli can cause your puppy to bark, as if it is asking you, "Hey, do you see this thing too?" It may also be guarding your home from that clearly villainous squirrel or neighborhood child, barking to frighten it away as well as warn you of its presence. While constant and loud barking can give you and your neighbors a headache, yelling at your puppy to be quiet will only sound like you are barking as well. Now the puppy really thinks it is doing the right thing because you have followed suit. Reacting to every whimper, yelp, and woof will only teach further neediness in your puppy. There is no cure for a barking dog because it is just what dogs do naturally, but you can train your dog to be calmer and not react in such an urgent matter.

Chewing

Your puppy should have all its baby teeth by the time you bring it home, but it will begin teething again at 4 or 5 months old when those teeth fall out and its adult teeth come in. You can expect excessive chewing to lessen the aches associated with teething, so provide many heavy-duty toys for your puppy to gnaw on. Be sure they are the appropriate size for your puppy. If they are too small they present a choking hazard, and if they are too large, your puppy cannot enjoy them. Some popular chew toys include the Kong Puppy Teething Dog Stick Toy, available at PetSmart, and Doctors Foster and Smith's Puppy Teething Rings.

Your puppy may want to gnaw on your hands as well as its toys. Do not allow your puppy to do this, and do not encourage the behavior by roughhousing with your bare hands. Always play with a toy so the puppy does not nip and bite at your hands. Failure to teach the puppy that your hands are not chew toys can result in unintentional aggression later on when it tries to initiate play and instead bites you or a family member's hand. A puppy that bites and chews does not mean you will have an aggressive dog — it just means your puppy has not learned the proper way to use its mouth and teeth, possibly from early separation from its canine family, or it is not being given an outlet to exercise its chewing needs.

It is debatable whether dogs gnaw on a sofa or destroy a pair of designer shoes out of spite. Those who are optimistic about dogs' intentions say they are simply chewing on an object because it carries their owners' scent. Dogs are also known to chew apart books, or whatever else they can get their teeth on, simply because they are frustrated or bored. Some cats also like to chew things, too. If you catch any pet chewing on something, always direct them to an appropriate toy. Just like a puppy, a kitten may chew things because it is teething.

There are taste-deterring products, the most popular being Grannick's Bitter Apple® spray, that you can spray on objects to deter your puppy from chewing them. It has a bitter taste that your puppy will not enjoy, but is completely harmless. However, some puppies seem to like the taste, so it may not be effective for your puppy.

Odd Puppy Behaviors

Obviously it will be nearly impossible for you to see any changes in your puppy's behavior because you have just brought it home and have not even learned the full range of its personality quirks. Your puppy still needs time to learn and explore before it develops a set personality. However, there are some behavioral issues that raise concerns and will either need training or a trip to the vet to diagnose and correct.

Excessive aggression

Canine aggression is a common complaint of pet behavior, and can have very serious or harmful results. Aggression is a threat or harmful action directed toward a group or individual. There are many reasons a dog may exhibit aggressive behavior, but aggression toward a human is dangerous and unacceptable.

Dominance aggression

Dominance aggression is used by dogs to gain and maintain a valuable resource, such as food, a bone, or a toy. This type of aggression may also arise when a dog is disturbed when resting, or when the dog is being led by the collar, groomed, or disciplined. The dog may exhibit body behavior such as a snarl, growl, direct stare, a high tail with quick stiff movement, or piloerection (hair standing). As a dog grows into maturity, this behavior may become more common between 1 and 3 years of age.

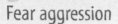

Fear aggression

Fear aggression is a behavior that dogs tend to show to other people, stimuli, or unfamiliar dogs. This fear may arise due to inadequate socialization, a genetic predisposition, or an adverse experience the dog may have had. This behavior may be exhibited toward men, children, an unfamiliar dog or noise, or the veterinarian. Often these dogs may try to escape the situation before exhibiting aggressive behavior.

Predatory aggression

Dogs are natural-born hunters and chasers. Predation is an instinctual behavior and involves stalking, chasing, catching, biting, killing, and eating prey. This type of aggression is more prominent in certain breeds, and can often be a very hard habit to break. These dogs may stalk and chase cats, children, birds, small pets, deer, or horses. Predatory aggression toward children or other pets is very dangerous or even fatal. This type of aggression can be very difficult to change and often carries a poor prognosis.

Territorial aggression

This type of aggression often occurs when a dog responds aggressively to unfamiliar animals or people that come into its territory. This can occur in the home, yard, or vehicle. These dogs try to appear larger by standing stiff-legged, ears and tail up, and with piloerection. They may also growl, bark, lunge, snap, and bite. This behavior also usually develops after sexual maturity between 1 and 3 years of age. This type of dog who always barks and lunges at the mailman "wins" every time because he or she drove off the intruder — really, the mailman just left. Remove these opportunities from the dog and desensitize it by introducing a variety of visitors. The dog may be placed in social isolation for this behavior, and needs to be adequately confined to prevent injury to people.

Puppies will mouth and put their jaws around anything and everything; this is completely normal. Like a human baby, your puppy is exploring its environment using its mouth. A puppy may accidentally bite too hard, but it usually is a genuine accident. Puppies learn how to use their mouths from their canine family. If your puppy is very young, it may not know how to behave, so you must teach it. However, it is not normal for a puppy to be overly aggressive, such as breaking the skin of its owner or baring its teeth. Something or someone has taught this puppy to be fearful and on edge when it is exposed to a certain stimuli. Puppies are especially sensitive as they are learning about their environment, so if something in their environment hurts them, they are likely to be aggressive toward it in the future. You will need to find the source of the fear and train the puppy not to fear the situation that is causing the aggression. You can contact a dog behavior specialist who can guide you through this process at the International Association of Animal Behavior Consultants. Their website is **www.iaabc.org**. Many owners do not mean to teach their dogs to fear a certain object and think it is even normal for an animal to fear loud appliances or moving objects, whether it is a vacuum or a lawnmower.

Case Study: Advice from the Author

My Dog Roscoe

My dog Roscoe was not fazed by anything. He would lie down on his little bed in our family room, minding his own business, and nothing ever scared him. When someone would vacuum, they would vacuum the room all around him until they needed to get to his area. They would turn off the vacuum and try to get him to move on his own, to tell and show him they needed to vacuum that area for a minute. He would get up nonplussed and watch the person vacuuming clean around his area, and then go back to lying down and napping like nothing happened. This same behavior would take place outside when he was relaxing in the grass. My dad would be mowing the lawn and have to stop to get him to move. Roscoe would get up, stand, and just watch him mow the lawn. When my dad was done, Roscoe would just go right back to where he was resting, not fazed at all. A couple times he would not even get up at first, but lift a paw as if to say, "All right, go ahead, I do not care."

Dogs will come to not fear these objects if they were never teased with it as a puppy. Roscoe disregarded the vacuum because it did not bother him and he was not taught to fear such appliances. Children will often use a vacuum, mop, broom, or other objects as a toy during play. If these objects are used during playtime with your puppy, it could become frightened because it is a foreign object, and your puppy may think the child is trying to hurt it with the object. What the owners do not realize is that they are torturing their puppy into thinking that a vacuum is a scary object that is out to get them, and the dog will learn to despise the appliance. As the dog grows up, it will go into a barking frenzy every time the vacuum is on because it has made enemies with it. If dogs do not have a reason to fear something, they will not act afraid or have other strange behaviors.

If fear is not the cause, it may have a neurological condition that is causing the aggression. This can include seizures or encephalitis (brain swelling), which cause abnormal changes in a dog's brain that can trigger many odd behaviors, including aggression. This is uncommon and can only be diagnosed by a vet, so do not jump to conclusions out of fear of the worst-case scenario. Even if something is wrong, your vet will be able to help you decide the best course of treatment.

Lethargy

Many breeds of puppies are naturally energetic while they are awake, so if your puppy seems lazy or listless this is not normal behavior. If your puppy exhibits any cold-like symptoms such as a temperature of 103 degrees Fahrenheit or more, harsh coughing, or vomiting in addition to lethargy, take it to the vet immediately, as a young puppy is not as strong as an adult and will likely need help getting better.

Lethargy is not the same as having a frightened or withdrawn puppy. Remember, your puppy just moved away from its mother and littermates and has your whole big house to adjust to. Being a little scared is normal, but completely ignoring everything to lie in bed all day is not.

Your Puppy's Love (and Other Emotions)

The same debate over whether cats have true emotions also exists for dogs, yet there are more emotions associated with dogs than any other animal. Young lovers are described as having puppy love, and the quality of loyalty is inextricably linked to canines — they are man's best friend. As we established with cats, this debate seems to be more about how similar dogs' emotions are to humans' and not a question of whether they have any emotions.

Primary emotions are those felt immediately and are instinctual, such as fear of a threatening situation. Other primary emotions include happiness, anger, and sadness, but all these primary emotions lead to more complex secondary emotions that we learn from society and experience. Think of the definition of an emotion like jealousy. It requires the being to understand that it is an individual and it wants something another individual has. An emotion like fear can result from pain, which is something the body recognizes naturally and does not require a true sense of self. Scientists claim that dogs cannot feel secondary emotions because they fail the mirror test — a test where the dog is shown its reflection and observed to see if it recognizes itself. In the past decade, this test and old ideas of self-awareness in animals has come under scrutiny, and scientists are revisiting the question, "Do animals have emotions?"

Alexandra Horowitz's article, "Disambiguating the 'guilty look': salient prompts to a familiar dog behavior," outlines a study where owners left their dog in a room with scientists and upon returning were told to either praise or scold their dogs for their behavior. Many times, the dogs did not perform any disobedient action, but the owners were informed they did and were told to scold them, and the dogs still appeared guilty. This lead the owners to believe their dogs really had disobeyed the scientists, so their dogs felt guilty because of it. In reality, the dogs were merely reflecting distress at their owner's actions such as yelling or finger brandishing, and did not genuinely display the guilt.

So how does all this scientific data relate to your adorable puppy looking up at you with such seemingly obvious adoration? Pet owners need to realize that they do not have any definite means of understanding their pet's emotions, so they may need to approach behavioral issues by thinking outside of the human box. Just like the examples of your cat appearing to show jealousy or spite, your puppy may appear to be feeling emotions that you recognize in human terms. While future studies may prove that dogs do feel secondary emotions, it is still too soon to assume your puppy really is feeling jealous or guilty the way a human would. Making assumptions about your puppy's emotions can lead to improper training for behaviors you have misunderstood.

The idea of science explaining emotions seems like an oxymoron to many people. Many pet owners vehemently disagree with the idea that their pets do not experience the more complex human emotions. They will swear that they have had their dog for years and have seen countless examples of emotions like pride, greed, or compassion. While this may be true, it is worth keeping an open mind and considering all possible causes of a dog's reaction and behavior. As a pet owner attempting to bring harmony to a house with an established cat and a new puppy, you are required to be the translator of your animals' emotions and not the projector of your own. No matter how much we love our pets, they are not humans and experience the world differently than we do.

Special Attention for Your Pets

Nowadays, there are many ways people award their pets with special attention, which may or may not be something for you. Pet owners throw celebrations for their animals for all sorts of occasions just like they would for a human. Your puppy may enjoy the attention and added socialization of a welcoming party, or you could pamper your cat with a special party that includes yummy but healthy treats. Your puppy is more likely to enjoy a house full of guests and people to play with, while your cat would probably prefer a more down-to-earth special occasion. These special parties are fun for owners and can provide a chance for your cat and puppy to spend some time apart, which might be needed after all this time getting acquainted.

Ideas for your puppy

🐾 Throw a birthday party. You can invite other dogs that are friendly to help socialize your dog, as well as give it extra attention from many people.

🐾 If your dog is a water-loving breed (like a Labrador), you can have a pool party with small, kiddy pools on a hot summer day.

🐾 Many dogs enjoy opening presents, so try wrapping up a treat inside a loosely wrapped package. Just be sure your dog does not eat any paper.

Ideas for your cat

🐾 Pamper your cat with special grooming. Does your cat love to be brushed? How about a good back scratch?

🐾 Cats love a tasty treat. Give your cat canned food or delicious treats — something special to show your love.

🐾 Buy your cat something fit for royalty like a plush cat bed, a continuously running drinking fountain, or deluxe cat furniture.

You are not the only person who will give your pets attention during their lifetime. Another trend that is gaining popularity is pet dating sites. These are websites where single pet owners go to meet other single pet owners or pet lovers. Some examples of these include PetPeopleMeet.com and DateMyPet.com. While this may sound silly at first, the idea behind them is an important one. If you are single, do not forget about your pets when searching for a partner. What if he or she is allergic? Is he or she going to be willing to help you care for your pets? You do not want to be caught between the needs of your partner and those of your pets. By finding a partner who shares your love of animals, your pets will have a loving home with plenty of attention. This will help your cat and dog stay on their best behavior, free from jealousy, anxiety, and boredom.

Continued Behavioral Issues

If your cat continues to run when the puppy comes into the room, even though they have been living together for some time, do not assume that your cat hates the puppy or that your cat is socially inept. It just shows that any stranger is still a stranger. That barrier will be broken once the cat gradually makes the decision to come out and explore on its own. It is important for you to allow your cat to set the pace and to only provide encouragement, not coercion, to interact with the puppy. Your cat will be uncomfortable and possibly hostile because it will not feel safe, which will only encourage more hiding. It should be tolerable to allow your cat to hide out as much as it wants and feel withdrawn for a while. Normally, the cat will exhibit this behavior for a few days, as the introduction of the new puppy may disrupt its routine and instill fear in the cat.

If the cat continues to hide away but is healthy, it is best to leave it alone. It will come out when it is good and ready. Forcing the cat out of hiding will only cause it to be more fearful of the situation. According to the Sacramento Society for the Prevention of Cruelty to Animals (SSPCA), you can try to desensitize your cat in this circumstance. Determine a distance where the cat can feel safe around the puppy, and give your cat tasty treats for being around the new animal.

The SSPCA also recommends that you do this at a gradual pace. Slowly move the new puppy closer to the cat and see how it responds. If this is done too quickly, you will need to start over from the beginning. Be sure to work in short sessions, and if necessary, consult the aid of a professional animal behavior specialist.

Your puppy may be just as frightened as your cat. If you want your puppy to learn to become more comfortable when the cat is around, start by getting your puppy to come out of its shell with you first. You are most likely not the one the puppy is uncomfortable with, but the main idea is you can have your puppy play with you while the cat is around to distract it and show that the cat will not be a bother. Get your pup's security and playfulness where it should be by incorporating special activities. To trust the cat, your puppy first has to trust you. After all, you would not pair up two animals if you knew they would be dangerous to each other, and once your puppy learns how to play nice from you, then it can show the cat that the puppy is not a danger either.

Even after a lengthy period of acclimation, your cat and puppy may still display fearful or aggressive behaviors toward each other. Certain behaviors will require training to eliminate, and the following chapter will outline specific ways you can get your cat and puppy to behave properly, as well as basic training all new puppies require. After all, you want an all-around, well-behaved puppy — not just a puppy that is good with your cat.

Case Study:

Other Tips on Behavior Issues

Gayle Ballinger, owner and head trainer
Pawsitive Steps Dog Training
Seattle, Washington

Your cat will notice you giving loving attention to the puppy, like you do with it. It is good for you to remember to show by example that the other pet is a friend as well. Learn to show each pet they are important and nothing will change that. Ballinger says that it is important that if you are petting one animal and giving them attention that you do not stop doing it the second you see the other animal, or worse, drop the attention from one and then turn around and give it to the other. Here you must continue to give the one attention and acknowledge the other, but it is important you do not allow one to push the other away from you. The cat and puppy are both equals in the home and are to be treated and seen this way. Show your pets what the acceptable behavior is by example. You have to watch how you are acting as well.

Teri Dickson, pet owner
Marathon, Florida

Dickson also recognized when her cats became very jealous of the newcomer and became more needy. The existing pets seem to want more attention from the owners as new pets join the family. It is like they need reassurance that their place is not being taken over by the newbie. Dickson recalls how her cats reacted when she brought a new puppy home. They would come up and stand in her lap and stare into her eyes as if saying about the dog, "Please, tell us she is not staying!"

Jeff Marginean, CEO
JEMAR Entertainment, Inc.
Host of the "My Buddy Butch" Radio Show
North Canton, Ohio

When dogs become stressed, there are many signals they will throw out that should alert the owner to a possible confrontation, including pacing, panting for seemingly no reason, gathering up all of the toys or chews to one area, or shifting the eyes to one side with head pointed forward. These signs indicate the pup is stressed out and fearful, and the actions indicate distrust about coming into a room for fear of meeting the cat. The supervised interaction is the only way to show them or train them that they are safe in the company of each other, Marginean said. Granted, your cat will still show signs of fear and hesitation even as you are happily playing with the puppy and showing the cat there is nothing to be afraid of. You do not know when your cat will come around and break out of its discomfort as of yet.

Myrna Milani, D.V.M
TippingPoint, Inc. / Bond Consulting Services
Charlestown, N.H.

How can you tell how your animals feel about each other? How can you be sure that everything is going well? Myrna Milani suggested being patient. As long as both are eating, drinking, and showing no evidence of stress-related medical problems, they are doing just fine. Studying your pets' daily habits and rituals can tell you how their behavior can change over a course of time. Some animals can accept a new addition in a matter of weeks. Others may take months or longer. Anything is possible. For some, it is love at first sight — Milani stressed that different pets will have different reactions. Your role as the pet owner is to address them separately before putting them together.

CHAPTER
7

Training Together

Beyond litter box training, which is usually taught to kittens by the mother cat, most pet owners do not train their cats. This is understandable, as cats are independent, self-reliant creatures, so there is usually no need to train them. However, you will need to train your new puppy to perform a number of actions, and it may benefit your cat and puppy's relationship to train them together. As mentioned in Chapter 1, cats can be trained using a clicker and positive reinforcement, just like dogs. Even if you do not necessarily want to train your cat to perform tricks, your cat will find the mental stimulation fun and challenging. Your cat will see you training your puppy, so giving your cat the equal opportunity to participate in this activity can help give it a greater sense of belonging and more friendly exposure to the puppy. If your cat has any unwanted aggressive behaviors, such as swatting, biting, or scratching, now is the perfect time to try to do away with them. You may even be able to train your cat to be nicer to your puppy by playing with your puppy in front of it. This way, your cat will see your interaction is friendly and positive, and it may learn that the puppy is not a threat.

The Key to Training

The key to all training is being consistent and persistent. Everyone in the house needs to speak the same cue words so the puppy can easily understand the command. Remember, even though it seems like it understands your speech at times, your puppy does not even hear your voice the way you do because of its ability to hear more frequencies than humans. According to Laura Hungerford, D.V.M., of the University of Nebraska, dogs hear noises up to 45 kHz, while humans only recognize sounds up to about 23 kHz. This means that dogs can hear and respond to sounds that humans may not even pick up.

Using uniform and simple cue words or phrases will help your puppy catch on to your desires quicker than if it had to learn to associate multiple, complicated cues with an action. Even if your puppy seems to have trouble catching on, do not change your training method unless you have exhausted it. Switching routines will not give the puppy enough time to learn — just be patient and stay positive. Your puppy will pick up on your frustrations and may become frustrated itself, so try to be a happy role model so it will enjoy training. These same ideas apply to training your cat, whether you want to teach it a trick or rid it of an unwanted behavior. Cats in particular will need persistence while in training because of their independent nature.

As mentioned in Myth No. 4 in Chapter 1, some dogs are capable of holding more than 150 words and phrases in memory. One word they need to hear frequently is their name. Use a new puppy's name often when you are together so it can learn it, especially when teaching new words and tricks. The pup will hear its name along with a command and your praise, and over time you will get the dog to be attentive to you when it hears its name. If your dog is purebred and has a long, complicated name on its papers, it is advisable to shorten what you call it down to a simple name. Although dogs do not recall certain instances where they learned something, they are able to respond well to names and commands. The words you use will only have meaning with the tone of voice in which they are spoken. You want to continue to tell your puppy that it is in fact a good boy or girl in a positive and upbeat tone, as well as have a stern voice to indicate it has performed an unwanted action. The right words with the right actions are important, but dogs rely mostly on the tones behind them.

Cats do not identify words with actions as dogs do, even though they have the ability to remember words, phrases, and their names. They do not usually answer to sit or stay commands because they are used to doing their own thing, but certain tones do help them associate events with feelings. For example, speaking calmly to a scared cat and saying it is all right when the new puppy is around shows that you are calm and they can be as well. Cats have a responsive system to certain sounds like dogs do. You can see a cat learning how certain sounds or tones correlate with an action to be performed, and it will respond a certain way as a result of the sound.

Chapter 6 discussed techniques for fixing behavioral issues by making the negative behavior undesirable to continue, such as urinating outside the litter box or chewing on objects that are not toys. These methods taught your pets that there are adverse reactions to performing these behaviors, which can be effective, but sometimes, craftier pets need more than simple deterrents. They need a positive effect connected with their acceptable actions, and no reaction associated with their negative actions. For example, when your cat eliminates in the litter box on a regular basis, award it with a treat. However, if your cat scratches up the living room couch, do not offer it any attention as you usually would.

Training Good Behavior

As with most mammals, puppies need to be taught how to behave. You need a firm understanding of your puppy's behavior and how to teach it what actions are acceptable with your cat. A well-trained puppy will become a happy and well-adjusted dog and have a much easier time living in peace with your cat. While many states allow puppies to be sold at 8 weeks old, this is still a crucial time in their development. Puppies learn valuable social skills from their play time with littermates, such as bite inhibition, so waiting to adopt a puppy until it is 10 or 12 weeks old can really make a difference in its behavior; just be sure that whoever was caring for the litter socialized your puppy with other humans or you may have a very frightened puppy on your hands. Puppies should still receive socialization and begin training even if they stay with their mother until 12 weeks of age; they just get the added benefit of more time learning how to be a dog.

Top 5 hard-to-train dogs

These dogs may be cute, but they are notoriously hard to train. Choose one of these with caution, and be aware that you will have to devote extra time to training.

1. Shih Tzu

2. Basset hound

3. Mastiff and beagle (tie)

4. Bloodhound

5. Pekingese

Source: *Dogs' Most Wanted: The Top 10 Book of Historic Hounds, Professional Pooches, and Canine Oddities* by Alexandra Powe Allred

Housebreaking and crate-training

Housebreaking tends to be the hardest behavior to train for most new dog owners. If puppies came housebroken, there would undoubtedly be even more dog households than the 45.6 million that currently exist in the United States, according to the APPA National Pet Owners Survey. People will tell you a variety of ways you can successfully house-train your puppy, but the best method is one that praises success and ignores accidents. Yes, ignores. Do not scold your puppy or punish it in any way when it goes to the bathroom inside.

Although previous training methods taught owners to stick a puppy's nose in its waste, use discretion and avoid harsh punishment techniques. This method is ineffective for several reasons. Puppies do not have the capacity to link previous actions with future repercussions, so unless you catch your puppy in the act it will not understand that you do not like the action of eliminating indoors. It may think you are mad at it for whatever action it was performing when you dragged it away to shove its nose in the waste. There is no way you can catch your puppy in the act every time, so you lose consistency with this type of training. Even if you could catch your puppy in the act every time, the aggressive action of pushing its head down will only teach your dog to fear you and possibly become afraid to go to the bathroom around you at all. This means it will seek out hidden areas where it feels safe going to the bathroom, and the only thing worse than finding a surprise is finding an old surprise.

Instead, focus on the behavior you do want through praise. When your puppy does go potty outside, praise it so much that you would be embarrassed if your neighbor saw you. Give the puppy especially tasty treats, lots of petting, and pitch your voice high while saying "good dog!" There is no way your puppy will not share in your enthusiasm and want to experience it again. When an accident occurs, do not make a fuss or scold your puppy. Simply clean it up with nothing more than a firm "no," if your puppy understands this cue. It might be a good idea to move the puppy out of the way while you are cleaning up after it so it does not witness you doing so. Puppies may think messes are acceptable because you will always clean them up. The goal is ignoring, not emphasizing, the unwanted behavior in any way. Keep in mind that even with a successfully trained dog, it is still capable of having accidents for a variety of reasons, such as fear of severe weather conditions or poor diet. Sometimes dogs will think that after you have been gone for a while, they are allowed to call their own shots. Anytime an accident occurs in the house, firmly tell it "no," and then immediately bring the dog outside.

Use a spray that is made to fully eliminate the smell of the accident so your puppy will not be attracted back to the same spot and use it again. If not, something strong like vinegar works as well to get the odor away. You should use baking soda on carpets to help soak up liquids. Simply sprinkle the baking soda on the wet spot, dab it up, and then clean with spray as usual. If you do not have special pet-stain sprays to clean up an accident, be very careful of any regular household products. You can use anything that is lemon or citrus scented. This is a scent that cats cannot stand and will be very unpleasant to them, therefore creating a negative association with the mess. Stores also will often have neutral-smelling sprays and cleaners that work for both pets.

Start your housebreaking training with realistic expectations. A puppy can only hold its bladder for a short amount of time; the general formula for how many hours a puppy can hold its bladder is its age in months plus one, but all puppies are unique, so it is better to observe your puppy and learn its abilities. If you leave your puppy alone for too long, it cannot help but have an accident. Help your puppy succeed by giving it minimum opportunities to fail. Take it outside frequently so it has plenty of chances to grow accustomed to the outdoors and feel safe eliminating there. Keep your puppy in areas with tile floor and gates, and cover carpeted areas with newspaper. You can even incorporate the smell of grass and soil in this area by filling a shallow litter box with turf, this way the entire area is all right to use as a bathroom. This would be especially helpful to puppies from the sporting and hound breeds, as they use their noses the most. House-training will take up a large portion of your day for a few weeks. This is a responsibility that comes with being a dog owner. Rushing through it will only result in ineffective training and setbacks in the process, so focus now and do it right the first time.

Soon you should notice that your puppy tends to use one area of the newspaper. Now you can begin crate training. The use of a crate to facilitate housebreaking will provide consistency and help to eliminate the chance of accidents. We discussed that dogs like crates when they are made into a place where the dog feels safe. This means you cannot force your puppy inside the crate and shut the door, expecting it to feel safe. You may have had to do this when it first met the cat, but now you have the opportunity to truly make the crate your puppy's safe and comfortable place. Allow your puppy to explore the crate on its own terms. Leave the door open, and place a few treats inside the crate. This will encourage your puppy to enter it willfully, as well as associate pleasant objects and experiences with the crate. If you see your puppy enter the crate, praise it verbally. Trying to reach in and pet it may encourage it to come back out.

Choose one spot to place the crate. This will become your dog's home base. Because dogs are instinctually pack animals, they need to feel a part of the activity and be able to visualize the other members. Place the crate in an area that is not isolated from daily activities. Placing the crate in a corner of the living room is often a good area for your dog to observe what is going on with the family. A puppy that is isolated in another part of the house will often seek attention through excessive barking or trying to escape to be with its "pack." Your puppy will be integrated into the family much faster if it can see, observe, hear, and smell all the day's experiences.

Make sure to place the crate in an area that receives adequate ventilation, so fresh air can flow freely around it. The space must be a comfortable resting temperature and not placed in direct sunlight because this may cause your dog to overheat, especially in the summer. A warm environment is especially critical to young puppies that sleep alone because they would normally be resting with their mother or siblings and sharing in their body warmth. Ambient temperature for young dogs, younger than 10 to 12 weeks of age, should be approximately 80-plus degrees. This can be accommodated with a warming sock or Snuggle Safe that can be heated in the microwave to maintain its heat for many hours and is safer than a heating pad that has cords or fabric that puppies may chew on.

The crate space provides not only your puppy a safety zone, but also your home. If you must leave the house for a period of time, you can securely put your puppy there and know there will be no chewing or destruction in your home. When you travel, the crate can be transported with you to new places, such as hotels or other friends' homes, and it gives the puppy a consistent familiar space. The crate gives you the control during house-training to deter accidents and the ability to praise the puppy when you are there when it properly relieves itself. When you are home and able to supervise the puppy, let it out with the family to participate in daily events and play. The crate is a tool and not a convenience factor for inadequate supervision. Keep the crate door open when your puppy is out of the crate so it always has access to the safety zone and resting place. You will find that your dog seeks the crate out when it wants to take a nap or even go into it to play with toys.

According to the HSUS, the philosophy behind crate training is creating a den for your puppy. This den creates a safe haven to rest or take shelter in during a bad storm. Along with keeping your new pet from accessing other household objects while in training, a crate provides a form of transportation for your puppy. The HSUS also cautions not to use the crate as a form of punishment. This will instill fear in your puppy, causing your puppy to no longer want to enter the crate. Also, make sure not to leave your puppy in the crate for extended periods of time. Puppies less than six months old should remain in the crate no longer than three to four hours at a time. Use the crate until you fully trust your puppy not to cause destruction in the house.

Because dogs are den animals, or animals that like to burrow in enclosed spaces, they are naturally inclined to cozy up in a crate. Like other den animals, dogs appreciate having their own space to cuddle up and rest in that is away from stress and the elements. The size of your dog's crate is important; it needs to be the perfect size to feel secure in times of stress — not too big or too small. Your dog will learn that its crate is its own personal space, and it will lay inside of it on its own without any coaxing from you.

About that circling habit ...

The size of your dog's house also needs to accommodate its quirks. You probably notice that your dog likes to circle around a few times before lying down. This is a behavior all dogs show — both domestic and wild. Scientists are not certain why dogs do this, but they do have a couple hunches. One theory is that the dog's ancestors did this to trample tall, unkempt grass and rid the ground of unwanted critters hiding there before lying down. Another hypothesis is that wild dogs like to sleep with their noses into the wind, so they turn in circles to find the wind. Either way, it is a dog's natural intuition to do this, and your dog's house should accommodate its natural desires.

Crates are rectangular cages made of sturdy wire, molded plastic, canvas, or soft-sided strong fabric. Molded plastic crates are very strong and easy to clean. They are held together by nuts and bolts, and come in a variety of colors. They are usually the least expensive way to maintain your dog's sleeping environment, and most are suitable for airline travel requirements. Wire crates provide a good 360-degree view of the environment, often have two doors for easy access, and can fold flat.

Wire crates have a more "open" feel and may not be appropriate for more shy or reserved dogs who may feel intimidated by all the open space. Most wire crates can be covered with special

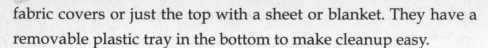
fabric covers or just the top with a sheet or blanket. They have a removable plastic tray in the bottom to make cleanup easy.

Canvas crates are lightweight and can be folded easily for travel. Soft-sided crates are appropriate for small and toy-size breeds. They are best suited for travel, may have a shoulder strap or wheels, and can be suitable for carry-on luggage on the airlines. The crate should be large enough for your dog to stand up and turn around, but not so large that it may want to eliminate waste at one end and sleep in the other.

Whether you choose a plastic crate or a fabric crate on a collapsible frame, there are four steps to crate training. First, introduce the puppy to the crate, leaving the door open to allow it to become comfortable with the space. Place the crate in an area of the home where the puppy spends the majority of its time, like the family room. Be sure to put a soft blanket or towel in the crate, and place treats in it to persuade your puppy to enter.

The second step in crate training is to feed your puppy its meals in the crate. The puppy will have a pleasant feeling associated with this space because it is receiving its meals here. Push the food dish further back into the crate for each feeding, until you see that the puppy is becoming more comfortable with its new space. Once you see the puppy remains in the crate and enjoys its meal at ease, close the crate door. Open it as soon as the puppy finishes eating.

The third step is to increase the length of the crating periods. Keep the puppy in the crate for short periods at a time while you are still home. Call it to the crate and reward it with a treat when it enters. Sit nearby for a few minutes with the crate door closed, and then head to another area of the house. Return to the crate, and observe the puppy quietly again for a few minutes before letting it out again. Continue this process several times, gradually increasing the time you are away from the puppy and the time it stays in the crate.

The last step is to leave your puppy crated for short time intervals while you are away from the house. This can be accomplished once your puppy is able to remain in the crate for 30 minutes without becoming afraid or anxious. Be sure to place treats and some safe toys with the puppy. Before you leave, your puppy can be crated anywhere between five to 20 minutes. Try varying the time intervals.

Do not drag out your departure. Keep your exits as prompt as possible, giving your puppy a treat and then leaving quietly. When you return, keep the reunion low-key to prevent a build-up of anxiety in your puppy. Keep crating your puppy even while you are home, so the puppy does not associate your departures and being left alone with crating.

Once the puppy feels comfortable around the crate, you can begin closing the door for short periods of time. Be sure to take your puppy outside before you do this. If you know it has been a while since it went potty, it is not a good time to try crating. Your puppy will likely cry at first when it is confined. Do not try to comfort it — this will only be interpreted as positive reinforcement for its whining. If your puppy continues to whine, you will need to determine whether it is a cry to eliminate, or if it is simply testing your patience. Use a phrase associated with elimination, such as "outside," and see how your puppy responds. If it becomes excited, you can take him outside. If not, then the best thing to do is ignore it. You should leave a toy in the crate so your puppy does not become bored. After some time passes, and only if your puppy calms down, you may let it out and immediately take it outside. This lets the puppy know it will always be given the opportunity to go potty after being crated so it does not feel as if it has to go in the crate. Dogs have a natural desire not to be near their waste, so your puppy will not want to relieve itself in the crate to begin with. This is also the reason the crate should not be overly large. If it is too big, your puppy will be tempted to go in the furthest corner and be free from the mess.

As your puppy gets better at holding its bladder, you can leave it in the crate for longer periods of time. If your puppy starts having more accidents, you have moved too quickly and need to take a step back with the training. Following these guidelines will help you potty train your puppy within a couple weeks. Remember to be consistent and persistent — the key to all pet training. Praise the positive behavior of going outside, and ignore or downplay unwanted indoor elimination. The best way to do this is newspapering the puppy's room or holding area, but it is unrealistic to think you will not have to clean up at least a few accidents.

Case Study: Advice from the Author

Roscoe as a Puppy

When my dog, Roscoe, was a puppy, I taught him to signal me when he needed to go outside. I took some bells and tied them on a string dangling from the blinds by our back deck. First I would take his paw and make him swipe it to make the bells ring, and then I would let him outside on the leash. After he went to the bathroom I would open the door and call to him to come in, and then on entering the house again give him a treat and tell him he was a good boy. I kept at this bell-ringing activity every time. Roscoe was let outside, but I only gave him a treat if

he was successful in going outside and not in the house. When he got older, I took away the bells to see how that would take effect, and Roscoe made his own substitute by pawing at the blinds on the door. They echoed throughout the house, and without even looking I figured out what he was telling me. It does not matter what noisemaking item is used as long as you recognize it as your puppy's signal that it is time to go outside.

After potty training

Do not get rid of your crate after potty training is over. Your puppy needs a place to retreat should it feel threatened, and it needs a comfy place to sleep. Once your puppy is housebroken, you can put that nice expensive bed inside the crate to give it a luxury den. If you find that it starts having accidents again after you add the bedding, you may have to remove it because your puppy has learned the material will absorb its urine.

Crates are also a good way to travel with your puppy since it is not safe to have a dog moving around inside the vehicle while you drive. Even after your puppy is fully crate-trained, you should not leave it shut in the crate any longer than need be, and definitely no longer than eight hours or overnight. If your family is very busy, you need to find another method of potty training, as it is unfair for your puppy to be cooped up all night as well as most of the day. Consider hiring a dog walker or having a neighbor visit while you are out for the day. Ideally, someone needs to be home for a good portion of the day or your puppy will get lonely and possibly destructive.

Barking

The problem with barking is that it is not always an undesired behavior. We like our dogs to bark with happiness when we play fetch in the backyard or if they are protecting our home from an intruder. We do not like it, however, when our dog barks incessantly at every person who comes to the door or barks at 6 a.m. because it is just so happy we are finally awake. Your cat will also dislike an overly boisterous puppy, so you must train it to be quiet when necessary. How can an owner be consistent with training if the behavior is not consistently good or bad? You can teach your puppy a command to stop barking, which focuses on rewarding your puppy's silence regardless of the circumstance.

When your puppy starts barking, grab some treats and walk over to it. Say "no bark" in a firm, clear voice. Briefly present the treat in front of your puppy, and then hide it. Since it cannot bark and eat at the same time it will stop barking, and you can praise it. Keep this pattern up until your puppy begins to associate the cue "no bark!" with rewards. Wait for your puppy to stop barking on cue, even if only for a few seconds, and then offer the treat and praise. Continue to extend the amount of time between the cue and the treat. With consistency and persistence, your puppy will understand to stop barking when you tell it to.

Yelling at your puppy or even talking to it in an attempt to calm the barking will only encourage the behavior. Your puppy will think you have joined in with its barking, so clearly it is doing the right thing. Repeat the "no bark" cue, and then ignore the puppy if it does not comply, or remove it from the room with the stimuli until it can calm down.

It will also help to cut your puppy off from certain stimuli that you know cause excessive barking. If it cannot help but bark at creatures in the backyard, close the blinds. Eventually you should be able to re-expose your puppy to more stimuli, but for now it may be too overwhelming for it to deal with and not bark. Sometimes, your puppy may be bored or lonely and bark to entertain itself or try to get you to interact with it. Make sure your puppy gets plenty of exercise and entertainment throughout the day so this does not happen.

You should be aware of why your puppy is barking at all times. Do not get in the habit of abusing your "no bark" powers. All dogs have a reason for barking, and if you do not know what the cause is, you may miss a very important message from your dog about its needs or even the safety of your home.

Biting

On some level, puppies explore their world with their mouths, which will inevitably lead to intentional or accidental biting. When a puppy hears its littermate yelp in pain from a bite it has inflicted, it learns that biting hurts and is not acceptable. It will also be nibbled on by its littermates, which will truly drive home the association of biting with pain. Do not teach your puppy that biting people is acceptable under any circumstance — even play. This can lead to accidental biting injuries in the future. Yelp just like another puppy would, say a simple verbal cue like "no bite," and walk away from your puppy if it does nip or bite you. This will teach your puppy that biting during play makes playtime end abruptly.

You can also encourage positive behavior by offering your puppy plenty of toys it can chew on. If it bites you, say "no bite," and give it a chew toy instead. Praise the puppy when it plays with the toy. Creating bite inhibition in your puppy will be vital to your cat's relationship with the puppy. It would take any cat a long time to trust an animal that has bitten it in the past.

Top 5 Most-Likely-to-Bite Dogs

These dogs are quick to snap, making them a bad choice for homes with young children.

1. Chow
2. Shih Tzu
3. Lhasa apso
4. Toy terriers
5. Dachshund

Source: *Dogs' Most Wanted: The Top 10 Book of Historic Hounds, Professional Pooches, and Canine Oddities* by Alexandra Powe Allred

Walking on a leash

Many new owners are surprised that they have to teach their puppy to walk on a leash. It just seems like a natural dog behavior, but in reality it is a learned one. Start training your puppy to walk on a leash as soon as possible, especially if you have a large breed. You want to be able to walk your dog, not be dragged by it. At first, you should use a simple 6-foot leash, not one of the retractable ones, because you want to have better control over how far your puppy wanders. You are going to start leash training indoors to minimize distractions and smells, so be sure you puppy has gone potty before you let it roam the house.

To begin, let your puppy examine the leash and eliminate any curiosity. Do not let it chew on the leash: Say "no bite" if it does, and remove the leash if necessary. If chewing on the leash remains a problem, try getting a lightweight metal chain as it will not appeal to the puppy like nylon or leather will. You can also use Grannick's Bitter Apple® spray. Your puppy will not like the sour taste of the spray, but this is only discouraging the behavior, not correcting it. You can use it as a temporary solution while you teach your puppy the cue "no bite."

After the puppy has examined the leash, clip it to its collar and let it drag it around the house for a little while. This will get it accustomed to the feel of the leash and show a frightened puppy that the leash will not hurt it. You can then begin walking around the house for a few minutes at a time holding the leash. Stop walking whenever the puppy pulls too hard on the leash in an attempt to lead you. Once the puppy becomes calm and the leash is slack because the puppy is no longer pulling, praise your puppy and continue walking. Increase the lengths of your walks over time, and then move to walking on a leash outdoors. There is no need to yank on your puppy's leash to make it stop pulling, just stop walking and wait patiently for it to let up. Pulling back or yanking your puppy's leash can hurt its throat and is aggressive behavior on your part. If you constantly stop when your puppy pulls on the leash, it will learn that walks stop when it does not walk at your pace. You can also encourage your puppy to pay attention to you instead of all the stimuli outside by bringing a few tasty treats that you disperse intermittently during the walk.

While on a walk ...

Many people who have yards or a lawn are very proud, and protective, of its beauty and maintenance. Dogs love to eat, roll on, play in, dig in, and eliminate on it. So, always be a good neighbor and do not let your dog eliminate on someone else's lawn when you take your dog out for a walk, and if it does happen, apologize and pick it up immediately. This is when plastic bags come in handy — always take a few with you on a walk. Urine contains nitrogen that can scald or "burn" lawns and leave unsightly brown or dead spots of grass. Female dogs can especially cause these burned spots because they squat and tend to put all their concentrated urine in one spot. Grasses such as fescue and perennial ryegrass are more tolerant of urine scald, while Bermuda grass and bluegrass are more sensitive. Clover, such as white clover or strawberry clover, are easy to maintain and are a good substitute for grass, require less water, require less fertilization, and can better tolerate the harsh effects of urine.

Teaching Cues

Teaching your puppy basic cues such as sit and stay will help you manage its behavior in any situation. Knowing that your puppy is obedient will help you introduce new activities and people to the dog without fearing it will react with bad behavior. All cues signal an action you want your puppy to perform, which it learns through repeated experience of hearing you speak the cue and then being rewarded. In a way you are tricking the puppy into performing the action, then the moment it complies, you reward and praise it so it will want to perform the action again of its own will.

You may substitute a different word or phrase for any of these cues. In fact, this is recommended if your puppy's name sounds like any of these commands, as you do not want to confuse it. So if your puppy's name is Jay, you might need to say "down" instead of "lay." Keep phrases clear and simple for maximum understanding, and remember that your puppy does not understand synonyms. If you normally say, "leave it" as a cue, suddenly switching to "no touch" will be ineffective.

Sit and lie down

When your puppy seems alert but not too hyper, try teaching the sit cue. Hold a treat in your hand and let your puppy smell it. Slowly bring your hand back over its head so it must look up to see the treat, which should cause its back end to lower and eventually touch the ground. The moment your puppy's behind touches the ground say "sit" followed by praise and the reward of the treat. Do this repeatedly until your puppy gets the concept of what sit means, and eventually you will not need to use the treat. Simply praising your puppy will be enough.

Teach your puppy to lie down after it learns to sit, as the two actions are related. Your puppy must lower its back end first to lie down, which is the first step to sitting. Perform the same movement with the treat as you did to teach sitting, but once your puppy sits, lower the treat to the ground so it will lower the front end of its body to get the treat. Your puppy may stand back up when you lower the treat; if this happens, just start over with "sit." It will learn what you are trying to convey after multiple tries. Once the puppy lies down successfully, immediately say "lie down" and give it the treat and praise, just as you did when you taught it to sit. Many owners say "lay" instead of "lie down," but lay sounds too close to "stay," so you may want to avoid the confusion — and be grammatically correct!

Stay and come

Teaching a puppy to sit and lie down is usually easy. Getting the puppy to stay can be much more frustrating, so stay consistent and be persistent. You might need to wait until your puppy is four months or older before the cue will stick because puppies have shorter attention spans.

Get something your puppy cannot resist, like tasty treats or its favorite toy. Set this item in front of your puppy but restrain it gently so it cannot get the item. You can hold your puppy's front legs or scruff it. Say "stay" and keep the puppy restrained for about three seconds while praising it. Praise your puppy only while it remains still, as it must associate the positive reward with being still. Then let it go to retrieve the item, which is the ultimate reward. Lengthen the amount of time the puppy must stay as it masters the cue. If your puppy tries to move too soon, repeat the cue. Do not let the puppy retrieve the desired item until it has stayed for the full amount of time.

Next, try telling your puppy to stay when there is no item. At first, stand right in front of your puppy until it stays frequently. Once it has followed your command, you can begin to walk away. Call it over to you, then tell it to stay and begin to walk away. If it tries to follow, repeat "stay." Eventually, you can ask it to stay and go out of its sight. When it obeys you, you can call the puppy to your side again. This will be the true test to see if your puppy understands what stay means. Some trainers suggest a release cue for the stay command, such as "okay" or "go," but often times you will use the stay cue to leave the house without the puppy trying to follow. How can you "release" the puppy when you have already left? It is against a dog's nature to stay still for a long period of time anyway, so the longest a dog will want to stay is about 30 seconds. Instead of a release cue, you can use "come" to reinstate action, which can also be a frustrating cue to teach.

Often, owners create situations where the puppy will not benefit from coming to the owner. For example, if your puppy takes a long time to come to you, do not scold it. You are rewarding its obedience with punishment instead of praise. Your puppy does not understand you are mad that it took too long to respond. Another mistake is only using the come cue to take the puppy away from a scenario it enjoys, such as when it is time to leave the dog park. The puppy will associate the cue with the end of fun and not want to respond. Instead, reward your puppy with

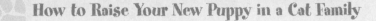

positive reinforcement when it does come to you with a treat, verbal praise, and petting. You can make a game out of the cue by having another person call the puppy after it has come to you. This will also help socialize and exercise your puppy.

Your puppy will learn to associate other noises and actions with fun activities, so you will rarely need to say "come" when it sees you head to the front door for a walk, or when it hears you opening its food container. It may help to praise your puppy when it figures these cues out and comes to you on its own by saying "good [name]." Then your puppy will learn that "come" often means you are going to do something enjoyable together. Never reprimand your puppy after it comes to you, even if the reason you called it over was to get it to stop an undesirable behavior. It has moved on from the behavior and focused on you, so punishment at this point will only be associated with being next to you. One way to train your puppy to come is to tempt it with food or treats. While extending food from your hand, tell the puppy to "come." Once it approaches you, praise it. Keep taking a few steps further back with food still in your hands, repeating the "come" command and waiting for your puppy to approach you. Lessen the food rewards once the puppy regularly responds to your commands. On average, a dog should get rewarded once for every five times it responds properly.

Drop it

The "drop it" cue should be taught for safety as well as obedience. What if your puppy picks up something dangerous? You cannot approach your puppy in an attempt to snatch the item because it will only encourage a game of keep-away. To train this cue, you will need two toys: one your puppy likes and one it loves. You can also use a treat instead of a loved toy since food is so tempting. Give your puppy the toy it likes, and let it play for about ten seconds, just long enough for it to really become focused on the toy. Then hold up the toy or treat your puppy loves, and as it drops the first toy say, "drop it." Then reward it by handing over the second toy or treat. Continue practicing this maneuver until your puppy will drop the first toy without seeing any reward. Remember to always verbally praise the correct reaction to this cue.

Your Relationship with Your Puppy

Some owners feel they are being mean when they enforce training because the puppy may protest during certain activities, like crate training. If you feel this way, remember that teaching these good behaviors and obedience keeps your dog, cat, family members, and home happy and safe. Your puppy is learning about the world through you and will come to trust you. The time you spend training your puppy is quality time that demonstrates your love, and as long as you focus on reinforcing positive behavior, your puppy will not think you are mean. You have built a relationship of trust and praise, so how could it?

Can you be strict about house rules and still make your puppy feel comfortable? Can you be fun but still enforce the proper discipline? It can be quite hard to stop or ignore certain behaviors because they are cute or make your little puppy seem so sad and pathetic, but remember all the problems that come with an untrained adult dog, such as jumping, biting, and incessant barking. Any

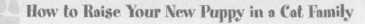

unmanageable behavior can lead to someone getting hurt, or worse, forced relinquishing of your dog. If it tries to play with someone and bites him or her, your dog may be taken from you and put down. If it barks all day and you live in an apartment or rent a house, the landlord can force you to give up your dog. Why cause yourself and your dog such grief when training can prevent these kinds of scenarios?

Training your puppy will also strengthen the bond between your cat and puppy. Cats appreciate a well-behaved puppy and will feel safer around a controllable puppy. If you have a breed with a strong prey drive, cues like stay and come can protect your cat from being chased. However, you cannot forget that cats can hurt a puppy as well. Your approach to training your cat will differ from training your puppy and may take longer because your cat is much more set in its ways.

Training Your Cat

Training your cat to perform certain actions is not only entertaining for you, but wonderful mental stimulation for your cat. According to the *Journal of Ethology*, an experiment showed that cats were able to distinguish between two or three circles in exchange for a food reward. If nothing else, this may offer some hope for people who believe their cat will be difficult to change.

Many cats are kept indoors, at least in metropolitan areas, and they do not get walks or potty breaks like dogs do. A bored cat will find ways to entertain itself, which are often destructive, such as clawing at furniture. Cats need to see training as a fun interaction with you because they are not as motivated to please like a dog is. Since training a cat to use a litter box is as simple as simply showing the cat the box and placing it in the box to scratch around, we will assume it knows how to use the litter box and stick to the fun activities. You can also visit Karen Pryor Clicker Training (**www.clickertraining.com**) and create a free profile to log in and view articles on clicker training for your cat and puppy.

Listening to a clicker

Karen Pryor's method of clicker training has shown great success with dogs and cats, as well as birds, horses, and other small animals like ferrets. It is very simple and only requires tasty treats and a clicker — a plastic holder with a piece of flexible metal that snaps to make a sharp click noise. This click noise will signal to your cat that it has performed the correct action, and receiving the treat immediately after will reassure it that it has done the right thing. The clicker provides a level of precision and consistency your voice cannot, which will help your cat catch on to the correct action much faster than trying to tell it when it is correct. The clicking sound is much more distinct and the cat can easily recognize it. You also use your voice for other interactions with your cat, while the clicker is only used to say, "good job, now you get a treat." Pryor suggests starting with target training, which is holding up an object (such as a pencil) for your cat to touch. The moment your cat touches the object, click your clicker and give your cat a treat. Cats are naturally curious, so getting your cat to touch the target with either its nose or paw should not be difficult. Just holding the object in front of the cat should be enough incentive for it to explore.

Try moving the target farther away from your cat to see if it truly understands the connection between touching the target and receiving the treat. Most cats catch on quickly and will enthusiastically bump against the target to get their reward. Keep mixing it up by moving the target around or adding obstacles to get to the target, like a box your cat has to maneuver around. This keeps the mental stimulation strong because your cat has some light problem-solving to do. This same target method of training will work for your puppy as well, so consider training your pets separately and then bringing them together so they can have quality time that is fun and rewarding.

If your puppy gets along fine with your cat, but your cat is still skittish, you can try clicker training to get it more comfortable with the puppy. Encourage your cat to approach your calm puppy, and if it does, sound a click and reward your cat. You can do this gradually, bringing it closer to the puppy every time. You could also make a target out of your puppy's belongings to get your cat comfortable with the puppy's smell.

Walking on a leash

Could you imagine not only taking your puppy for a walk but also your cat? Many owners give their cats the freedom to come along for a walk in a safe way by training them to walk with a harness and leash. Teaching this skill will take immense patience, and you cannot expect your cat to catch on like your puppy. Cats have a tendency to be more restless and want to wiggle their way out of a harness when going for a walk. They need more emotional reassurance from their owners.

You must get your cat acquainted with the harness, leash, and everything that is outside. This is easily overwhelming for a cat, so take your time. First, purchase a harness and leash designed specifically for cats. This will provide maximum comfort and keep your cat from escaping. Cat harnesses and leashes are available at most pet stores, and specialty harnesses are available on websites such as Crazy K Farm Pet and Poultry Products (**www .kittyholster.com**) and HDW Enterprises, Inc. (**www.hdw-inc .com/walkingjackets.htm**). These specialized cat harnesses cover a wider area of the cat's body with no thin straps that put pressure on the cat's neck and belly.

Most cats can begin leash training successfully between 6 and 7 months old. Once you purchase the harness and leash, leave them somewhere for your cat to sniff and explore them on its own, so it can learn they are harmless. Keep the harness and leash away from the puppy though, as your cat will likely ignore them once they are covered in slobber. After your cat has had ample time, put just the harness on your cat. If it does not like it, leave it on for five minutes and then give it a break. Increase the time gradually, all while encouraging your cat to move around and become accustomed to the feeling of the harness. Once it has adjusted to that, add the leash. Do not hold the leash just yet, but let your cat drag it around and get used to it at its own pace. Make sure your puppy is put away for this, because a dragging leash is an irresistible toy to chase.

Now you can introduce your cat to the outdoors. Some cats that have been kept indoors most of their lives will find this quite scary, so you must be patient. Try going outside when it is quiet so there are fewer noises to frighten your cat. It is recommended that you carry your cat outside for the first time to ease its initial fears. Leash training can be an excruciatingly long process but may provide your cat with many benefits such as exercise, mental stimulation, and special time with you. Giving your cat a special outlet for frustration and boredom, such as taking a walk, can be enough to eliminate most unwanted behaviors such as scratching and over-vocalizing.

Much like a dog, your cat will likely want to stop for extended periods of time and check out enclosed spaces like bushes and underneath cars. Let it do this as much as is safely possible. Never drag your cat on the harness — this will guarantee your cat will never learn how to walk while restrained. Do not punish your cat for being a cat and proceed only at the pace it is comfortable with. If your cat is naturally very shy, it may never enjoy a walk on a leash.

Case Study:

The Best Training Advice

Teri Dickson, pet owner
Marathon, Florida

It was almost as if Dickson's cats thought the dog's training was incorrect, and they were thinking they had to fix it and show the dog the right way. Sometimes Dickson's cats would look as if they were in complete disapproval of some action the puppy was taking. For instance, when her new puppy came home, the cats would follow along behind her in the yard and bury her poop like they thought she should know how to do that on her own. The cats were trying to show the dog how they clean up after themselves by mimicking their litter box activity. The cats saw the dog's way of doing its business as wrong and felt better setting it right.

Shawn Messonnier, D.V.M.
Paws & Claws Animal Hospital, Plano, Texas
One of the matters that dogs in particular need to understand is who the leader is. The human in charge of the situation must always be looked at like a leader by all of the pets. If you cannot establish this, then there will be little harmony and the animals will continue to fight, Messonnier said. You can work on the fighting issues by introducing them to mutually pleasing circumstances. In addition, you must quickly and constantly break up any fights that may start when you are around.

Kim Young, pet owner
San Antonio, Texas
Your new puppy is going to want to run all over the place to explore its new home and will not have the best understanding of boundaries and designated spaces. Teaching the puppy to stay out of the cat's space will be a challenge, and teaching the puppy to stay out of the off-limit rooms in the house is also going to be a task. Young said because dogs are pack animals, they do not like limits on where they can and cannot go. Young explained that her dogs feel the need to be around her all the time, which should not always be taken as an insecure act but a loving one that dogs enjoy your company. A cat will not understand this at first and will run when a puppy innocently follows it around. The cat knows the puppy cannot get it in its own room, so it retreats there. Young's cats have their own special room and have the choice of spending time in there or in common places with the dog. Eventually they came out once they learned to accept the dog as another member of the family. The pets grow to understand and respect each other's space.

Babette Gladstein, D.V.M.
New York, New York
Only bring the cat's food out when the cat is present — the same goes for the dog — to enforce the right possession of food. You can incorporate this as a teaching method and watch the animals to make sure that they would stick to their own food bowl and no one else's. According to Gladstein, your pets should have their own rooms and bowls there, but you can monitor their behaviors right in front of you with this exercise. Try feeding both animals in the same room at the same time but in different spots in the room.

For example, you can feed the cat on a counter while a dog may continue to eat from a dish on the floor. Here, they will both be occupied with their own food and know that the other pet is as well so they can eat at ease. When they are finished, remove the bowls right away. You can put them back in their own rooms at a later time so your pets know they can always rely on their food being there at all times — and they trust the other pet.

Sassafras Lowrey, pet owner
New York, New York

Sassafras Lowrey strongly believes in crate training for a dog. This is one of the most important aspects of training for a young dog other than socialization. Lowrey points out that crate training helps break the dog into the home. That not only helps train the dog, but is helpful regarding the cat as well. Your cat has it own room and can hide, and it provides more comfort to the cat that the puppy will have a place to be secured until it can be broken into the house successfully. On another plus side, the crate gives the puppy its own sense of security. Providing a dog or puppy with a crate where it feels safe, calm, and secure is essential for having dogs and cats coexist with each other, explains Lowrey. Lowrey explains that it is part of our responsibility to provide them with that to make the coexisting of three species — human, canine, and feline — a success.

Laurie Luck, pet owner
Woodbine, Maryland

Laurie Luck encourages others to be proactive by teaching their puppy some basic skills, because this is the key to good dog-cat relations. Luck gives an example of how she trained puppies. She taught them to touch her hand upon request, using the cue "touch," to distract the puppy when the cat comes around. Luck says if practiced every time the cat comes into the room, the pup will begin to look to you to play the game every time kitty comes near. This creates a solution to a problem long before it ever exists.

Debbie and Eric Margerum, pet owners
Vincennes, Indiana

The Margerums stressed how they kept a new puppy under the most restrictions, because it was in training, using a crate in the housebreaking process with the dog. Now that they do not lock the dog in the crate anymore, it will often choose on its own to sleep there. The dog eventually became trained so it was able to sleep with the Margerums and now has the choice to either sleep in its own bed or stay with the Margerums for the night. Their past cats had chosen to sleep with them while the new puppy was in its crate.

CHAPTER

8

The Health of Your Cat and Puppy

This chapter is meant to serve as a guideline for what you need to know about your pets' health. This is not meant to be a substitute in any way for the consult of a veterinarian, but instead it will give you the scope of health issues that can affect your pets and what you can begin to do to keep your pets healthy.

There is no way your cat and puppy can get along if they are ill. This chapter will help you learn the signs of specific illnesses, first discussing the common medical procedures that apply to cats and dogs and reasons why they are done. When your pets are young, you will no doubt make your first visit to the vet, and here you will have a chance to be updated on all the important medicines and vaccines that concern your pet's health. Staying on top of your pets' general and advanced health care will help you provide the best care for all of them. It is one of the most important aspects of caring for both a cat and a dog.

Spaying and Neutering

Spaying or neutering is not a cruel procedure. Until the pet population is under control, spaying or neutering your pets is a vital procedure. Have female cats and dogs spayed before their first heat cycle, usually at 6 months of age, and males neutered before they reach 6 months old. Talk to your vet about how old your pet should be to perform this procedure, as individual factors come into play, such as special health conditions and individual growth rate. Spaying or neutering provides health benefits that intact pets do not have, such as a highly decreased risk of cancer in the ovaries, mammary glands, and prostate. Many pet professionals recommend spaying and neutering because the procedure can help prevent diseases. Spaying decreases females' chances of having mammary cancer and also decreases the chance of pyometra, which is a severe and deadly infection of the uterine tract that is brought on by a female's heat cycles. Neutering males puts an end to prostate problems such as an enlarged prostate and cancer. It also prevents perianal adenomas, which are growth structures that form around the exterior of the anus.

Vaccines

Vaccination practices, such as the need for yearly booster shots, are coming into question. Many times, shots are unnecessary because the pet is not at risk for certain conditions covered by these vaccines. Many times, combination shots, a mixture of up to seven different vaccines, are given to cats and dogs. There are arguments for and against this method of delivering vaccines. Some vets claim that unless the vaccines are given all at once, the immune system will not respond to the vaccines until a few days later. Others say that an animal can develop autoimmune diseases, where the body attacks itself from being bombarded with so many dissimilar antigens. Antigens are what make vaccines work by compelling the immune system to produce antibodies that in turn make the disease harmless to the vaccinated animal. Many vaccinations also prevent diseases for a much longer period of time than previously thought. Some even last a lifetime. Instead of assuming revaccination is necessary, a titer test can be performed to see if there are enough antibodies in your pet's blood. This test helps prevent your pet from receiving unnecessary shots, as well as eliminates the potential health risks brought on by vaccinations. This blood test can be conducted by a veterinarian and can be performed for any vaccine, but it must be done separately for each one, as the needed concentration of antibodies varies for each disease.

It is hard to find clear-cut information about vaccines because it is such a profitable industry. Pharmaceutical companies make billions creating vaccines because they are guaranteed to sell — do you not want to protect a loved one, whether it is a pet or another

human? Your vet may continue to use outdated practices when it comes to vaccinations, so do your research to keep up with current information. You may even want to get a second opinion from another reputable veterinarian. If your vet seems like her or she is pressuring you into getting a vaccine for your pet, especially one you know your pet will have almost no chance of exposure to, you may need to find another vet. Some examples of shots that are not required annually include parvo, distemper, or kennel cough. There is no need to get a vaccine for a disease your pet will have limited exposure to, especially since all of the negative effects vaccines can produce are not yet known. Here are some factors to consider before vaccinating your cat or puppy:

- **Age:** If a kitten or puppy is vaccinated too early, it will not be protected. This is because the mother's milk has natural antibodies it passes to offspring. These antibodies will attack the vaccine and destroy it.

- **Health:** If your pet is sick you should not vaccinate. Its body is already working to fight off an infection or disease, and giving it more to deal with will likely lead to adverse reactions or vaccine failure.

- **Location:** If you do not live in an area that hosts the disease the vaccine prevents, there is no need to get it. While this seems logical, many vets do not mention that a certain disease is virtually nonexistent in your area.

Sometimes vaccines fail to work. The most common reason is the presence of the mother's antibodies. Your puppy could also come into contact with the disease before the vaccine has time to stimulate the immune system to create enough antibodies. Most vaccines take at least a few days, if not weeks, to work. There are also some infrequent causes of vaccine failure, such as incorrect administration methods, such as if the vaccine is meant to be injected in the muscle and instead was injected under the skin; a damaged vaccine from incorrect handling; or incorrect spacing between vaccines — too long or too short a time can be equally damaging.

There are concerns about cats developing sarcomas, cancer in the connective tissues and bones, as a result of repeated vaccinations. Vaccine creators are working on different types of vaccines that may decrease this risk, but for now the vaccines prevent more diseases than they cause and should be administered after learning which ones are needed. This information is not meant to dissuade you from vaccinating your pet. It is to give you as much information as possible, so you realize that your pets may still have a chance at becoming ill; do not ignore symptoms because you think it is impossible for your pet to get sick just because it has been vaccinated. It is also a reminder to find a good vet whom you trust to have your pets' best interest at heart, as well as a complete understanding of the newest vaccine procedures.

Dangers of Socializing Your Dog

Many people want to show off their newest family member to other dog-loving souls and will often take their puppies to public places, like a park or dog park. This sounds like a good idea at first, but bear in mind the dangers you may be unknowingly exposing your puppy to.

Parks are areas where a lot of unknown dogs have been with unknown vaccine histories. This exposes your puppy to diseases, such as parvovirus, which may exist in the environment for five years, unaffected by sunshine or freezing. What you do not know or cannot see may hurt your puppy. Socialization is valuable for all dogs, but be cautious about your choice of environment and the age of your dog. Puppies younger than 4 months are most at risk because their immune systems are not fully mature. This is why it is so important to protect your puppy with "puppyhood" vaccinations to build its immunity to this devastating disease. Make sure that whoever handles your puppy has not already handled other infected or carrier dogs, or what other dogs your puppy contacts are healthy. Do not feel panicked or threatened, just informed about who and what touches your puppy.

Rabies

According to an article by Jesse Blanton in the *Journal of the American Veterinary Medical Association*, "Domestic species accounted for 6.9 percent of all rabid animals reported in the United States in 2008," which includes cattle and livestock. Although rabies is rare in domestic animals, with 93 of every 100 cases of rabies in the

U.S. occurring among wild animals, most states still require all cats and dogs to have annual rabies shots. This is because humans can contract the disease, and it is deadly if left untreated. Rabies is passed on from infected animals, usually raccoons, skunks, bats, or foxes, through bites and scratches that leave an open wound. The aftermath of the infection causes either the animal to become vicious and aggressive or paralyzed in the neck. The first rabies vaccine is given around 4 to 6 months of age, and after this, they can be given annually or every three years, depending on which type of vaccine was administered.

The rabies vaccine has fallen under much controversy due to reported adverse reactions and the fact that owners feel the vaccine is unnecessary because the disease is so rare. Talk to your vet about alternatives and possible exemptions if you are worried about harmful reactions. If you notice facial swelling, vomiting, or fever up to 48 hours after your pet has been vaccinated, you should call your vet immediately. These may be signs of a severe allergic reaction.

Lyme disease

Lyme disease, an infection caused from bacterium, is contracted from ticks, most often the deer tick. In dogs, this disease can cause kidney problems when it has been present for a long time. It can also cause joint pain and inflammation. However, cats and dogs may not seem to show any symptoms of infection. Humans can also contract Lyme disease but display symptoms such as a fever and rash around the tick bite. Humans cannot get Lyme disease from dogs; they can only get it from infected ticks. Lyme disease is most common in the northeastern part of the U.S.

There is a vaccine for Lyme disease, but it is not very effective and should only be given to dogs in areas where the disease is highly prevalent. The vaccine should not be given to a dog that already has Lyme disease. This is because your dog's body has a memory of Lyme organism proteins, and by injecting them again you are only introducing more of these proteins into their immune system. Lyme disease is treated with an antibiotic called doxycycline for a 30-day period.

In humans, 85 percent of Lyme disease cases occurred in the Eastern portion of the U.S., 10 percent in Wisconsin and Minnesota, and 4 percent in California. Less than 1 percent of the cases were accounted for by all other states.

Cats: FVRCP

FVRCP is a combination vaccine for three different diseases: feline viral rhinotracheitis (FVR), calicivirus, and panleukopenia (feline distemper). Your cat probably got this vaccine as a kitten, and then again at 1 year of age. After that the vaccine is "boosted" with another shot every three years. FVR and calicivirus are upper respiratory viruses that produce cold-like symptoms and are highly contagious, but the symptoms usually vanish within seven to ten days. Rhinotracheitis, also known as feline herpes, stays in the body and can reoccur throughout a cat's life when triggered by stressful events, while the calicivirus seems to leave the body after a few months. Even though these viruses are very contagious, only cats that are placed in shelters or kennels have much risk of contracting either virus.

Panleukopenia is another story. A cat with this disease will lose its appetite, have vomiting and diarrhea, and have a low number of white blood cells, resulting in blood clot. It is widespread and hard to kill, although cleaning with a solution of one part bleach to 32 parts water may cause the virus to inactivate. The virus can survive on objects such as food dishes or litter boxes for years. It is most commonly spread to other cats by contact with an infected cat's urine or feces or any place the waste was located. Panleukopenia is often fatal, especially in kittens. The infected cat must be taken to a veterinary hospital, and can only be helped to feel better with intravenous fluids to prevent dehydration and antibiotics. Statistics are bleak for cats that get this disease, with 90 percent of kittens dying and 50 percent of older animals.

Cats: Feline leukemia (FeLV) and feline immunodeficiency virus (FIV)

Feline Leukemia (FeLV) and feline immunodeficiency virus (FIV) are retroviruses that are incurable and are spread to other cats through open wounds and bodily fluids. All cats should be tested for both of these viruses before coming into a new home. If your cat is FeLV or FIV positive, it cannot spread it to your new puppy, only other cats. Infected cats are a great danger to outdoor cats and a main reason why so many people are against letting cats roam freely. Feline leukemia can only survive outside an infected cat for a few hours, and a cat must be bitten or exposed to the virus for an extended period of time to contract it. A cat may be contagious two to three days before showing any symptoms. Once exposed to FeLV, a cat may be able to fight off the virus, it may become ill immediately, or may not show signs for years after exposure. This all is dependent upon the cat's level of immunity and the length of exposure to the virus. There are many vaccines against FeLV,

and it is recommended that all cats older than 4 to 6 weeks be vaccinated.

Cats with FIV (feline AIDS) often have many other health problems such as mouth infections, respiratory infections, anemia, swollen lymph nodes, and ear infections. They can live for many years with proper care, which will vary from cat to cat as the virus presents different problems from case to case. Many cats do not present any symptoms for years after acquiring the virus but will continue to spread it. While there is a vaccine, it causes all subsequent FIV tests to come out positive, so it is much harder to diagnose if the cat is infected. It is also not recommended by the American Association of Feline Practitioners (AAFP). The AAFP says it is likely that fewer than 82 percent of cats that receive vaccinations will be fully protected from the numerous FIV genetic variants present in nature.

Dogs: DHLPPC

Your puppy will likely receive a combination vaccine like DHLPPC every two weeks from 8 to 16 weeks of age. Your puppy having to undergo repeated exposures of short-duration vaccines may cause skin disease, autoimmune disease, allergies, and in the worst scenario, death. Talk to your vet about what is best for your puppy.

Here is what each letter of the vaccination name stands for as well as a description of the viruses: A three-letter abbreviation in parenthesis after the vaccination name is simply the full-virus name abbreviation:

1. **Distemper (CDV):** Spread by coughing or body secretions. This virus begins with cold-like symptoms and may progress

to neurological symptoms, like seizures. Distemper is often fatal. It occurs most often in puppies under 6 months old. There is no cure or any definite means of testing if a dog has the virus or has overcome it. Luckily, it cannot live outside a dog's body for long.

2. **Hepatitis (ICH):** Caused by the canine adenovirus type 1 (CAV-1). Canine adenovirus type 2 (CAV-2) causes a type of kennel cough and may also be treated by the DHLPPC vaccine. The virus is spread by contact with an infected dog's waste and affects the eyes, causing them to appear clouded or bluish in color. It can also damage the kidneys and liver. There is no cure and it may cause death in as little as two hours, especially in dogs under 1 year old. It may cause little more than a fever in other dogs.

3. **Leptospirosis:** There are several strains of this disease that exist mostly in tropical and subtropical climates. All of them affect humans as well but do not spread from human to human. Leptospirosis spreads through contact with infected urine or bite wounds or contact with stagnant, contaminated water. Symptoms include fever, anorexia, and possibly jaundice. It can be deadly as it can cause severe kidney and liver damage. The vaccine lasts less than a year, so if your dog is at high risk for this disease because other dogs in your area have the disease, it may need to be vaccinated twice a year.

4. **Parainfluenza:** Commonly referred to as kennel cough. The virus often goes away on its own, but small puppies or immune-compromised dogs are at risk for it developing into

something more serious. The tell-tale symptom is a hacking cough that may even sound like attempted vomiting. The vaccine for parainfluenza usually lessens the symptoms of the virus but is not very effective at preventing it. Pneumonia may occur with more serious versions of influenza, but this can be remedied with proper amounts of fluids.

According to the American Veterinary Medical Association, treating the milder form of this virus can be accomplished by providing your puppy with good nutrition and proper care to build up its immune response.

5. **Parvovirus (CPV):** Also referred to as "parvo." This virus causes bloody and severe diarrhea and vomiting. A vet needs to test for the virus for confirmation, as these symptoms could also indicate another illness, such as Lyme disease or an oral ulcer. These symptoms cause dehydration, which could kill the dog, especially small puppies. Parvovirus is extremely contagious, as it is spread through close contact settings, such as a kennel. It also seems to target Labradors, Doberman pinschers, and Rottweilers more so than other breeds. These and other black and tan breeds are more susceptible to this virus and are more likely not to recover.

6. **Coronavirus (CCV):** Similar to parvovirus in that it causes diarrhea, although not usually vomiting. With proper fluid treatment to stave off dehydration, the virus is not usually fatal.

There are variations of this vaccine, such as DHPP. Again, the controversy of over-vaccination applies to this vaccine. Some components can provide life-long immunity while others may offer less than a year's worth of protection. For example, the leptospirosis portion only protects for about eight months while the coronavirus portion does not require yearly boosters.

Parasites

Parasites are organisms that use the body of a host — in this case, your cat or dog — as a means of continuing their lives. Parasites can be deadly if left untreated and are easy to contract. Prevention is the best way to deal with parasites because many can reinfest your pet if you do not treat your entire home with proper cleaning procedures.

The Companion Animal Parasite Council (CAPC) is a good resource for pet owners to learn more about parasites that can infect their pets and can be transferred to humans. Visit the CAPC's website at **www. petsandparasites.org**. *Zoonotic diseases are discussed under the "Pet Owner Health" subheading of this chapter.*

The following is a list of tips to help prevent the spread of infection to you and your family, according to the CAPC.

1. Wash your hands thoroughly after gardening or dealing with raw meat.

2. Make sure meat is well-cooked before eating.

3. Wash fruits and vegetables to avoid contamination.

4. Monitor infants and young children sitting on the floor. Do not allow them to consume dirt or particles from the floor.

5. Retrieve animal feces from the yard daily.

6. Cover play areas such as sandboxes to shield from stray contamination.

7. Make sure your pet sees a veterinarian on a regular basis. Have it tested for parasites annually.

8. Deworm your pets based on your vet's recommendations.

9. Keep toxocara infections and parasites under control by administering products throughout the year, as directed by your veterinarian.

Heartworms

Heartworms are a type of roundworm that find their way into the heart and lungs after passing through mosquito bites. Heartworms prefer to stay in the pulmonary arteries of pets. Although dogs are more susceptible to heartworms because they have larger arteries, cats can contract them as well. Symptoms of heartworms include chronic inflammation, heart scarring, pulmonary vessels, and cardiac enlargement. Heartworms cause heart failure in the right side of the heart and could easily lead to death. Prevention is key when dealing with heartworms because the symptoms, such as chest pain, coughing, and severe damage to internal organs, are hard to detect. Heartworms can be prevented with small chewable tablets you give your dog once a month. Vets recommend getting a negative heartworm test before administering any variety of heartworm preventives. This test will determine any allergies your pet may have and if it will have a reaction to tablets.

According to the American Heartworm Society, there are some topical preventives should this be the cause with your puppy.

These products, along with the chewable tablets, have become increasingly popular in use due to their ability to kill developing heartworm larvae. Using the preventive on a monthly basis will eliminate the chances of infection. Consult with your veterinarian to find the appropriate product for your pet.

Intestinal worms

Hookworms, tapeworms, and roundworms (also called nematodes) are all intestinal parasites that can affect your cat or dog. Each type of worm has several different species, but for simplicity's sake, they will be referred to as a whole because symptoms and treatments are similar. Hookworms get their name from "hooking" their mouths onto the small intestinal lining. There are numerous ways for your pets to get hookworms: eating another animal that hosts them, eating soil or water that has hookworms present, or through larvae entering the skin. After larvae are coughed up and swallowed, the hookworms travel through the bloodstream and enter the lungs. Several larvae attach to the intestinal walls, while some move onto muscles and other tissues. Hookworms feed on blood, so anemia is the chief health concern. Check for pale gums, especially if your pet is vomiting or has diarrhea.

Tapeworms are flat and shed parts of the segmented bodies to reproduce. This causes rice-like pieces to appear in your pets' waste or around the anus and is usually the only symptom of infection. They can grow up to eight inches in length if left untreated. Your pet may get tapeworms from accidentally eating a flea with tapeworm larvae inside it or any other means of ingesting the larvae. Sometimes adult tapeworms detach from the intestine and move into the stomach, which causes the animal to vomit it

up. Tapeworms are only diagnosed visually, so take care to notice them and seek treatment. A large number of tapeworms can cause weight loss in your pet, which can be very serious.

Roundworms are the most dangerous to your pet. They cause the stomach to appear pot-bellied and can amass in great enough numbers to block your pets' intestines, which will cause death. Roundworms can infect your pet the same way hookworms do, but are much larger and look like spaghetti. All these worms can be killed with regular deworming procedures at the vet. Deworrming is recommended because of how easy it is to contract worms; puppies as young as 2 weeks old may be dewormed.

Coccidiosis and giardiasis

Coccidiosis and giardiasis are also caused by intestinal parasites, but they are single-celled organisms and not worms. Both are spread through contact with feces or contaminated soil (coccidiosis) or water (giardiasis) and both cause diarrhea. Coccidiosis is more aggressive and may even cause the death of small kittens and puppies. Keep your animals away from areas where other cats and dogs eliminate to prevent infection. The treatment for coccidiosis does not kill the organism but instead halts its reproduction, so it may take a while to cure. A drug treatment over one to three weeks is normally required in order to be fully effective. To treat giardiasis, medications such as metronidazole, quinacrine, and nitazoxanide can be used.

Fleas, ticks, and mites

Fleas can hop onto your cat or dog anytime they are outside, and they are active year-round in most places. One could even be on your pant leg when you come in the door and then transfer to the comfortable fur of your pet. Fleabites are very itchy and will cause your pet to scratch, and you will probably get a few bites as well. While having fleas is not fatal, they can transfer other parasites and diseases, such as worms and the plague. Although fleas are small and difficult to see, the bites are hard to miss and so is the "flea dirt" they leave on your pet — the black specks of their droppings that can be picked off your pet. There are numerous topical medications to prevent fleas in cats and dogs. Be sure not to mix up your cat and dog's flea medication, as the higher dosage of insecticide in the dog formula can kill your cat. There is also concern about the safety of certain flea control medications.

Safe flea control

Fleas can be a household nightmare. If they get into the home, they will get in all the soft fabrics and bedding and become a real hassle to get rid of. Not only will they bite pets, they will bite humans as well. According to the National Resources Defense Council (NRDC), nearly 90 percent of U.S. families use pet pesticides. Some products are safer than others, but many of these products create harmful chemical residues that linger on pet fur and in the home. Additionally, the NRDC says these pesticides remain on animal fur for several weeks. This may pose potential risks to family members who interact with the pet, as well as the pet itself. The levels of pesticide are almost 1,000 times higher than the levels deemed acceptable by the Environmental Protection Agency (EPA). This amount of toxic chemicals may cause cancer, brain damage, and serious nervous system disorders.

A paper released by the NRDC in April 2009 said that two

chemicals commonly found in flea collars are particularly dangerous: tetrachlorvinphos and propoxur, which are two of the most lethal pesticides still legally available. The danger extends beyond the pets to owners as well. If you have children who play with pets, they can get these chemicals on their hands, and if they touch their mouth or eyes prior to washing them, they may accidentally introduce poison into their bodies. This NRDC study suggested the following hints on protecting your pets and your family from these chemicals:

- Bathe pets weekly with pesticide-free pet shampoos, rather than using chemical-ridden flea collars.

- Use flea combs between baths.

- Launder pets' bedding in hot water.

- Vacuum carpets daily to eliminate hidden flea eggs.

- If you still want a chemical flea control product, discuss alternatives with your vet. For example, consider using the kind that is dispensed in pill form. They are less toxic and do not leave chemical residue on animal fur.

- Check the labels of the flea and tick control products before you purchase them. Avoid products that list tetrachlorvinphos or propoxur as the active ingredients.

- Also avoid permethrin-based products and those containing the chemical amitraz.

- For a comprehensive list of brand-name pet products, their ingredients, and the corresponding health risks, refer to Green Paws, which can be visited online at **www.greenpaws.org**.

Ticks do not infest animals like fleas do. Usually, one tick will imbed itself in your cat's or dog's skin and stay there to feed on your pet's blood. Ticks live in heavily wooded areas, so any pet that ventures outside into these areas is at risk for picking up a few. Ticks are harder to find because of this lack of movement and small number. Ticks can cause Lyme disease, tapeworms, and Rocky Mountain spotted fever. An organism known as *R. rickettsi* will impact certain dog breeds more than others. The majority of dogs will have a fever within five days of contraction. Other symptoms, such as depression, lethargy, and blood in the urine may occur. Ticks need to be removed carefully with tweezers to ensure their entire body is pulled from the skin. If the tick's head is still lodged in the skin, try to grab and remove as much as you can. Do not worry if you cannot take it all out, because your pet's immune system will try to pressure it out by creation of an infection site or tiny abscess. The same medications that prevent fleas often prevent ticks as well.

Mites are even smaller than fleas and ticks and infest the hairless areas of your pet, mostly the ears or skin. Ear mites will cause your pets' ears to become crusty and irritated, and they could become infected from constant scratching. Mites also cause a condition known as mange, which refers to how matted and raggedy the infected animal's fur becomes. The animal also suffers hair loss, as mites infect the skin and cause the hair to fall out. Demodectic mange, often referred to as "demodex," is the most common form of mange in dogs. This often is present when a dog has an immature immune system. The disease is prevalent in dogs younger than 12 to 18 months of age. Luckily, the illness is not contagious. Demodex mites live in the hair follicles. Cheyletiella mites live beneath dead skin cells, and when they move the skin appears to crawl, giving this condition the nickname "walking dandruff." Sarcoptic mange, or scabies, causes severe itching from the burrowing mites. Mites are often misdiagnosed as allergies because the symptoms are identical. Vets should perform a skin scrape to diagnose mites. An antiparasitic medication like ivermectin will be prescribed to kill them.

Pica

Although you may think your animal eating non-food objects is just an odd behavior, pica can cause serious health complications. Pica is a mental disorder that causes animals to want to eat non-food items. Experts are not sure why animals do this, but if your pet starts eating or licking odd objects, like string or plastic bags, you need to keep these items away from it to immediately stop this behavior. An object could get lodged in your pet's throat or form an intestinal blockage that is painful or even fatal. Waste has to be eliminated, and if it cannot pass the blockage, your pet will literally be poisoned by its own waste or suffer an intestinal rupture. Surgery will be necessary to remove the blockage, which is costly and can be avoided simply by keeping these items away from your pet. Another way to prevent your puppy from chewing on odd objects is to keep its chew toys scattered around the home so it will not have to search for an alternative.

There are two main theories behind pica behaviors: The animal is trying to make up for lacking a certain nutrient, or it is attracted to items because they are enjoyable to eat for a number of reasons, such as they are made from animal products that your pet can smell.

Obesity

Obesity is a very common problem for cats and dogs and is primarily caused by free feeding and lack of exercise. Feeding too many treats can cause obesity, as can providing people food, often in the form of table scraps, because it has more carbohydrates and fats than dog and cat food. If you choose to offer your puppy some of your leftovers, be sure this does not exceed 5 percent to 10 percent of the amount of calories needed daily. Obesity can lead to serious heart problems as well as diabetes and arthritis even if the dog or cat is still young. Sometimes owners dismiss a couple of extra pounds, but consider the size of your pet: If you have a small dog, a couple pounds can be a good portion of its body weight. For example, a six-pound dog only requires 50 calories per pound a day. You can tell if your dog is overweight if its ribs cannot be felt easily or if it has a noticeable tummy pouch. The tuck normally visible in the puppy's hind cannot be seen in an overweight dog.

Blame it on Genetics

Dogs are opportunistic omnivores if left to find for food themselves. This means that they will eat whatever they can, whenever they can. Domestic dogs are descendents of the gray wolf. Dr. David Mech, one of the world's most respected experts on the wolf, noted that an 80-pound wolf can eat up to 22 pounds of meat in one session, or may fast up to six months. A wolf's diet is primarily meat, almost all protein with some fat.

Diet is a major factor in your puppy's health and proper growth. Puppy foods are specially formulated with the proper balance of calcium and phosphorous to ensure proper bone development. This is why you should always feed puppy food and not adult food to puppies. Puppies can begin eating some solid foods as early as 4 weeks of age. Feeding puppy food should continue through the growth of your puppy, usually finishing by about 9 to 12 months old, depending on breed. Breed considerations are important in determining the amount of food your puppy eats or calories it needs. The energy needs per pound of body weight of a Pomeranian are twice that of the needs of a Great Dane.

According to research conducted by The University of Liverpool's Small Animal Teaching Hospital, diets full of fiber and high in protein are best for overweight dogs, because this creates a sense of fullness and is best for satisfying your dog. The research also found this diet to be beneficial for digestion. Talk to your vet to decide on the best feeding plan for your pet to prevent obesity.

Additionally, be sure to play with and exercise your pet so its mind can be kept off the decreased food intake.

If your cat or dog has a big appetite and always eats all its food, you may think this means it is hungry and you are not giving it enough to eat. No one wants to make his or her pets go hungry. However, the pet is usually getting plenty to eat. For puppies, they should be getting about 1 cup per 10 pounds of their body weight, and adult dogs should get 1 cup per 20 pounds of their weight. Cats should get a quarter cup of food per 5 pounds of their body weight.

Cats are carnivores. Therefore, their diet should mainly consist of meat. If you choose to give your cat a homemade diet, it should consist of 60 percent protein, 30 percent grains, and 10 percent vegetables. Acceptable forms of meat include fish, chicken, turkey, and beef. For grains, feed your cat brown or white rice. Leafy green vegetables are easy to digest and are beneficial to your cat's health. Always consult with your veterinarian before administering a homemade diet.

Puppies and dogs are more likely to have obesity issues than cats, and many times, owners do not realize their dog is overweight. Owners may develop a tendency to overfeed their puppy and not give it an adequate amount of exercise proportionate to its eating habits. Obesity in dogs could lead to a serious condition known as hypothyroidism, which is a deficiency of the thyroid hormone production. This disease is caused when the dog is fed normal amounts of food but is still experiencing obesity, and from this, the dog has a slower metabolism and a tendency toward a secondary skin disease, causing thickening, discoloration, and excessive black pigment in the skin of the groin, in addition to the weight gain. If you notice a big change in weight gain in your puppy and you sense it may have a thyroid condition, talk to your vet about the specifics of your puppy's diet and behaviors. Also see if a blood test can be conducted. Be prepared to go through a treatment of thyroid hormone supplementation.

Exercise Needs

Many cat owners do not realize their cats need to be active and get exercise. They are seen as animals that lounge about, but they were built to hunt and kill prey. All cats need exercise, so just because your cat is no longer a kitten does not mean it can sit around all day. If you need some ways to get your cat moving, there are many toys that are inexpensive or even free.

- **Boxes:** Cats love boxes. Cats enjoy being enclosed in small spaces because it provides them with a sense of warmth and protection from predators. You can toss a toy into the box for it to chase or cut holes in the sides to provide multiple entryways.

- **Catnip:** If you cat is fond of this, get it some catnip-stuffed toys or sprinkle lose catnip around its scratching post. There are even bubbles infused with catnip for double the fun.

- **Fishing pole:** These are easy to make but also widely available for purchase. Just get a dowel rod and tie a string to the end. Then tie feathers to the end of the string and watch your cat try to attack it when you dangle it in front of its face.

🐾 **Exercise wheel:** Yes, there are wheels for cats just like the those for hamsters and gerbils. These can get pretty pricey though, and you may have to train your cat to use it. Your cat will develop strong, toned muscles and a healthy heart, and it will be mentally stimulated. You can purchase cat wheels online from the Cat Wheel Company at **www .catwheelcompany.com**.

🐾 **Enclosures:** These provide your cat with limited access to the outdoors by enclosing them in a small space, such as a fence or tunnel made of redwood, where they can walk through and still enjoy the outside air. They get the excitement of seeing what is going on outside but cannot escape the yard or attack any small critters. Habitat Haven sells outdoor enclosures for cats at **www.habitathaven.com**.

Most puppies are incredibly energetic regardless of breed. Playing with your new puppy throughout the day will help keep it fit, as well as help it sleep through the night. Make sure your puppy does not become dehydrated and that its blood sugar does not drop too low, as many puppies will keep playing as long as you are willing, regardless of how exhausted they become. Excessive panting and pale gums are signs of overexertion and need to be addressed immediately with rest, water, and food. Do not forget your puppy's training during playtime. If it is normally not all right to jump on people, it is still not all right to jump on people during playtime.

When your cat and puppy are together, the puppy has to be reminded of how to behave indoors. Chase should not be encouraged, as it could get out of hand and turn into aggressive behavior, even though the pup may or may not be aggressive. Make use of your space outside in the yard as much as possible to help your puppy channel its energy and allow it to learn that this special space is used for running around freely. Practice simple but light rough play in the house with the puppy's toys. To prevent your puppy from creating destruction in the house, provide chewing toys as well as rubber toys to throw and chase. You want your puppy to see its toys and recognize them as things to play with. You want your puppy to grow up knowing what it can play with and what it cannot.

Pet owners often get a fenced yard for their dog, and you should consider this especially if you have a puppy that will grow into an energetic adult dog, like a golden retriever. All dogs love to run around and get exercise, but some breeds truly need to stay active to be healthy and happy. Fenced backyards are a safe security for the dog to run around freely without the worries of it running away. However, this does not mean you can leave your dog unattended. Many dogs are stolen right out of their owner's yards, especially purebred dogs. One solution to this problem could be attaching your puppy to a retractable leash. This leash will ensure that the puppy cannot run away, but at the same time, give it ample room to roam around your yard. Another option is to simply go outside and watch your dog, while getting fresh air for yourself at the same time. Many dogs also enjoy digging, which means they could escape if left alone for even a short amount of time. Be sure to provide some kind of shelter for your puppy outside so it has the option to get out of direct sunlight, like a mini doghouse.

---

10 Best Cities for Pet Lovers

You do not have to live in one of these pet-friendly spots to bring home a pet for your family, but these areas combine green space and good weather that make many pets — and their owners — happy.

1. Ellicot City, Maryland
2. Rocky Point, New York
3. Auburn, Alabama
4. Butte, Montana
5. Yankton, South Dakota
6. Lewiston, Idaho
7. Glasgow, Kentucky
8. Aiken, South Carolina
9. Flower Mound, Texas
10. Wolf Trap, Virginia

Source: U.S. News & World Report, August 2009.

Dental Needs

Cats and dogs need to have their teeth cared for just like humans do. Many owners are unaware of this fact, but a lack of dental care can lead to periodontal disease. This will make eating painful for your pet and could even lead to major health problems from bacteria entering the bloodstream through abscesses between the

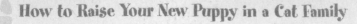
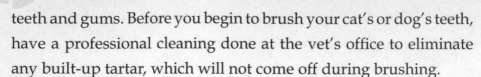
teeth and gums. Before you begin to brush your cat's or dog's teeth, have a professional cleaning done at the vet's office to eliminate any built-up tartar, which will not come off during brushing.

The veterinary technician uses hand instruments to scrape off the tartar buildup above and below the gum line. Fluoride paste is used afterward to smooth out the teeth and prevent future tartar development. You can help your pets' teeth stay healthy by brushing them at home — daily if possible. There are special toothpastes for cats and dogs that are edible and flavored to appeal to them. Do not use toothpaste made for humans as your pets will eat it, and humans' toothpastes are not edible. In dogs, ingestion of toothpaste may cause vomiting or loss of coordination.

Your cat and puppy will not be accustomed to having their teeth brushed, so you will have to introduce the procedure to them slowly so they learn to like it. Start by putting something tasty, like tuna water or beef bullion, on your finger and offer it to your pet. See how much your pet will let you touch its teeth over a few sessions like this, and remember there is no need to rush. You want your pet to like getting its teeth cleaned, and forcing it will not accomplish this.

Once your pet does not mind you massaging its teeth and gums, switch to toothpaste. You may have to backtrack a little to get your pet adjusted to the paste's texture and flavor. Apply a small amount of toothpaste to your finger and allow your puppy to lick it. If it is accepting of the flavor, rub some paste onto its canine teeth with your finger. Once it is ready, introduce the toothbrush. The bristles will be a very odd sensation for your pet, so again it may take some backtracking to get it used to the feel. Allow your dog to lick the toothpaste off the bristles so it gets used to the texture. If your pet only lets you brush a few teeth at first, that is fine. Let your pet set the pace, and soon it will look forward to having a clean mouth. In addition to brushing your pets' teeth, there are also many treats on the market that help scrape plaque and promote healthy teeth, such as Greenies®, which are available at **www.greenies.com**. Follow the directions on the packaging to be sure you do not overfeed your pets, as these treats are not the same as others.

Pet Owner Health

While investing so much time and care into your pets, do not forget about your own health. Many people suffer from allergies, and this is a common reason families give up their new puppy. They did not know a family member was allergic and do not know what else to do besides give up the puppy. Although there are some health problems you can catch from your cat or dog, owning pets is actually good for your health — so long as you take good care of them physically and emotionally.

Allergies

Have you or one of your family members noticed symptoms such as itchy and watery eyes or a runny nose since the puppy arrived? This can be a heartbreaking discovery made all too late by many pet owners. Allergies can develop at any point in a person's lifetime, so even if someone is not allergic to dogs as a child, they can be allergic as an adult. Before you decide to give up your new puppy, try adjusting your lifestyle to minimize the allergens and see if these suggestions alleviate the symptoms. These suggestions apply to cats as well, but it is unlikely an old cat will cause new allergies. First you need to find out if it is the dander (dead skin cells) or saliva that you or your family member is allergic to. If it is only the saliva, have that person wash their hands thoroughly after petting the animal, and obviously do not allow it to lick that person. If it is the dander, try these suggestions:

- Keep the pet off the furniture, especially if it is cloth.

- Replace any carpeting with tile. If this is not possible, vacuum daily.

- Purchase a HEPA (high efficiency particulate air) filter. This alone is enough for many with mild allergies. HEPA filters capture a large amount of tiny particles that vacuums usually retrieve and circulate back into the home. They can range from $10 to $50. Life expectancies vary for these filters, depending on the size of the room it is used for and the amount of particles it removes. It is recommended to replace the filter once or twice a year.

- Bathe your pet weekly to wash off the dander.

- Brush your pet daily or every few days. Ideally, have someone not allergic to dander do this.

- Feed your pet a sufficient amount of fat to keep its skin healthy. Dog treats containing omega-3 and fatty acids, such as Yummy Chummies Dog Treats, help your puppy maintain healthy skin and a shiny coat.

🐾 Always wash hands after handling the pet or pet's objects.

🐾 Keep your pet out of the bedroom completely. This is the room where people often spend the most time.

🐾 If the allergies are severe enough, talk to your doctor about medication options, such as Zyrtec, Singulair, and Claritin.

There are also a number of light bulbs on the market that claim to purify air. The anion light bulb is a compact fluorescent with a built-in ionizer. It produces significantly less ozone than an air cleaner and also provides illumination. It saves up to 80 percent of energy costs, lasts for up to 10,000 hours — eight times longer than an incandescent bulb — provides 100 watts of illumination, and can remove pet dander, smoke, pollution, pollen, dust, dust mites, and odors from surrounding air. These bulbs are more cost-effective than HEPA filters, as they not only trap airborne particles, but also destroy harmful bacteria, smoke, and odors. There are a number of manufacturers of these bulbs, and the average cost runs about $17 for one or $30 for two. One manufacturer is O-ZONELite™, whose bulbs provide over 6,000 hours of light and eliminate odors and bacteria in the air.

Top 5 Dogs for Families with Allergies

These dogs are not exactly hypoallergenic, but they do have a lower likelihood of causing allergic reactions than other dogs.

1. Soft-coated wheaten terrier
2. Basenji
3. Boston terrier
4. Chinese crested (hairless)
5. Schnauzer (standard and miniature)

Source: *Dogs' Most Wanted: The Top 10 Book of Historic Hounds, Professional Pooches, and Canine Oddities* by Alexandra Powe Allred

Zoonotic diseases

There are some diseases and parasites that you and your family could contract from your cat or dog; these are called zoonotic diseases. Thankfully all are treatable and not usually life threatening. However, if someone in your home has problems with their immune system, these conditions can be much more serious. The list below covers the most common zoonotic diseases in the United States that come from cats and dogs. Owning other pets or living on a farm exposes you to many more. For the most part, good hygiene will prevent these diseases and infections. Thoroughly cooking and cleaning food is important as well, as you are more likely to contract these diseases from handling your food improperly.

Ringworm: Ringworm is a fungal infection, not a parasite as the name implies. You can get it by touching your pet if it has the infection. It often creates a rash in the shape of a ring, and if it affects your scalp or beard, it could cause a circle of hair to fall out. Ringworm may appear as flat, round patches on other areas of the body. When ringworm affects the groin area, this is caused by fungus and is commonly called jock itch. On the feet, it is called athlete's foot. It is very contagious, and you can even spread it to other parts of your body. Keep ringworm infections covered to prevent this. Ringworm often clears up with over-the-counter powders or creams, such as Micatin, Tinactin, or Lamisil. Be sure to go to the doctor if it does not clear up within four weeks or appears infected.

Toxoplasmosis: Cats can get toxoplasmosis from eating small animals or raw meat and in turn give it to you when you clean the litter box. Any contact with cat feces could potentially expose you. It is caused by a microscopic parasite and often presents no symptoms in humans. Humans can contract it by eating undercooked meat containing the parasite or coming into contact with soil containing stool from an infected cat. However, pregnant women may pass toxoplasmosis to their babies who then can suffer from impaired vision, seizures, and mental problems. Always wash your hands thoroughly after cleaning the litter box or any activity that brings you in contact with cat feces.

Bartonellosis (cat scratch fever): Like the common name suggests, this bacteria can enter through a cat scratch or bite and cause infection. Cats get the bacteria from fleas. Lymph node swelling and possibly drainage can occur, as well as a general weakened feeling. Usually the infection is uneventful and clears

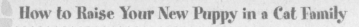

up by itself, but antibiotics may be needed.

Campylobacteriosis: Bacteria that can be spread by either your cat's or dog's feces can cause campylobacteriosis. Symptoms include diarrhea, cramps, and fever, but usually pass within a week. Some people do develop Guillain-Barré syndrome, an autoimmune disease that makes the body attack the nerves, which then causes paralysis.

Cryptosporidiosis: While more commonly contracted from contaminated water, research now shows that cat and dog feces can spread crypto. This organism causes diarrhea in humans, as well as nausea, weight loss, and fever. It is a tough organism with an outer shell that protects it from many water treatment methods, including chlorine. See a doctor if you suspect you have cryptosporidiosis. Oral treatments include metronidazole and paromomycin. In healthy individuals, the infection will clear up but may last up to a month.

Leptospirosis: Leptospirosis is spread through contaminated water and soil and causes general flu-like symptoms in humans. It can worse and cause organ failure that causes death. Even if your puppy received its DHLPPC, where the "L" stands for leptospirosis, it can still have the disease present in its urine and give it to you should you come into contact with it. Also, humans can contract this when their mucuous membrane or skin abrasions come into contact with environmental sources. If your puppy is actually going to grow up to help work on a farm by herding livestock, it is at an increased risk for this disease. Cats rarely catch leptospirosis.

Coxiella burnetii (Q fever): Q fever results from bacteria that are more commonly present in livestock but have been reported in cats and dogs. Q fever is highly contagious to humans, though rarely fatal. It causes a very high fever, vomiting, confusion, and chills, and can lead to pneumonia. The treatment is doxycycline, but can take weeks to fully heal the patient. According to the Centers for Disease Control and Prevention (CDC), humans can come into contact with this disease by inhaling organisms from infected barnyard animals' milk, urine, and feces. Rare forms of contraction include drinking contaminated milk or being bitten by ticks.

Worms and protozoa: All the intestinal worms and protozoa (single-celled organisms) mentioned earlier are zoonotic. However, many of the strains that commonly infect cats and dogs are not as likely to infect humans. Symptoms are the same in humans, sometimes more pronounced, and are treated with similar medications. Be sure to wash your hands and deworm your pets to prevent worms.

Fleas, ticks, and mites: While these external parasites often favor your pets, they will land and settle on you as well. While they can be incredibly itchy, they are not fatal, but they can give you other serious diseases, such as Lyme disease and Rocky Mountain spotted fever. Having pets increases exposure to these pests, so keep them on preventive medications.

Rabies: Rabies in the U.S. is extremely rare. Rabies is virtually nonexistent in dogs nowadays, so even though it is possible you could catch rabies if bitten by a rabid dog, the chances of encountering one are slim. Nevertheless, stay away from dogs that appear aggressive to avoid bites, and if you are bitten, visit a doctor immediately.

Do pet owners live longer?

There is much evidence to support that owning a pet helps people live longer and healthier lives. The simple action of petting a cat or dog lowers blood pressure, which is good for the heart. Children who were exposed to two or more dogs or cats as babies are half as likely to suffer from common indoor and outdoor allergies — including pet dander, dust mites, ragweed, or grass — than children who grew up in pet-free homes, according to research conducted at the Medical College of Georgia. In the study, headed by Dennis Ownby, M.D., pediatrician and head of the college's department of allergy and immunology, researchers tracked a group of children from birth to about age 7 to determine whether having a pet impacted their experience with allergies. Other studies have shown a similar decrease in asthma for children who live in homes with pets. People do not have to put up fronts or act politely in front of their pets, which allows them to unwind at home but still have companionship.

A study in *The Medical Journal of Australia*, conducted by the School of Veterinary Medicine at Rakuno Gakuen University in Japan, explored how pets affect human stress levels and emotions. Researcher Masahiko Motooka states, "We know that compared with people without a pet, people who keep a pet have been reported to adapt more quickly to stress associated with bereavement and other adverse events, require fewer visits to the doctor, and have stronger emotional stability and maintain a generally sounder state of health."

This indicates that pets help their owners through times of grief, such as the death of a family member. Research also indicates this benefit is strongest in children and teenagers who often have trouble expressing themselves to adults. Seventy percent of kids say that they confide in their pets when they are worried, scared, or have secrets because they feel like their pets are trustworthy and love them no matter what, according to a study by Alan Beck, Ph.D., at the Purdue University Center for the Animal-Human Bond. Another study, conducted in 1985 at the University of Michigan, showed that 75 percent of children between ages 10 and 14 turned to their pets for comfort when they felt upset. When parents rated their children's anxiety and withdrawal, kids who turned to pets for comfort fared better than children who did not draw on their pets for support or did not have pets.

The elderly seem to have the most evidence of increased life span with pet ownership. Pets can give seniors an increased sense of purpose because the animal depends on them for food and care. Elderly pet owners also get more exercise, which helps maintain their health. Whether it is a walk with their dog or an extra trip to the store to get some cat food, these people move around more and are thus healthier.

Dogs are also used for therapeutic purposes. People who suffer from seizures sometimes discover that their dogs can sense when a seizure is going to occur and can warn them. Some dogs will pull or push their owners to get their attention, giving them ample time to lie down to avoid injuries from a fall. If trained properly, some dogs could even bring their owners pillows or the telephone to call for help. While these dogs can be trained to bring items, there is no way to train a dog to sense seizures. Dogs can also help people with type 1 diabetes and can be trained to wake their owners during the night should their blood sugar fall too low. The dogs are relentless, and will bark, lick, and nudge until their owner awakes and gets his or her medication. The organization Dogs4Diabetics trains dogs for this purpose and gives them free to diabetics who apply for them on their website, **www.dogs4diabetics.com**.

Case Study:

The Most Important Thing about Your Pets' Health

Najela Cobb, pet owner
Victorville, California
In order to have a harmonious household, you need to be aware that the dog and cat do not operate the same — they may be treated equally, but they are treated differently. Cobb said the most important aspect of caring for two different kinds of pets is learning their different needs on an individual level. Through the basics you will begin to grasp this concept easily, and as they grow up you will be able to pinpoint special qualities they have.

Sassafras Lowrey, pet owner
New York, New York
Sassafras Lowrey stressed the most important thing to consider when caring for two different kinds of pets is remembering that they are very different. What sets a dog and cat apart mainly is that dogs generally require more training and exercise. Many people find them to be more high maintenance because of these additional physical needs. This is something that some self-identified cat people may struggle to adjust to, and a cat family learning to raise a dog will find it to be the most challenging.

Teri Dickson, pet owner
Marathon, Florida
Dickson talked about how you can incorporate a schedule for your pets and how this saves your home from falling into disorder and chaos.

Dickson explained that you have to be prepared for a little extra time to care for them, describing her daily routine with her animals. She takes the dogs out first thing in the morning and lets the cats in while the dogs are out. She feeds the cats inside, while the dogs eat outside, so each has its space to eat comfortably. Dickson also makes sure that both the cats and dogs get one-on-one time with her separately for individual bonding time.

Debbie and Eric Margerum, pet owners
Vincennes, Indiana
Dogs have a lot of limitless energy that comes naturally. Providing a dog with a way to channel this energy will help in the long run. A way to calm down a particularly energetic puppy is to give it time to go outside and run around all it wants. The Margerums have a dog that is part Labrador, and they know that this kind of dog needs more exercise than usual. They compare this need to hyper children needing to get out and play. Once the puppy gets its exercise, it is much happier, and then it can relax when it comes inside with the cat. If you ensure your puppy fulfills its exercise needs, it will be less likely to bother the cat.

The Margerums found it difficult to keep their cat and dog from eating each other's food. The cats were curious about the dog's food but not as much as the dog loved the cats' food. The Margerums explained that a dog is likely to eat anything that smells good, and cat food has such a rich aroma, which can be hard for a dog to resist. Their dog had diarrhea as a result, demonstrating how a pet eating the wrong food could also lead to illness. This example also has pointed out that food that smells and tastes good leads to another problem: the feces also smelling and tasting good. The Margerum family soon figured out why they did not have to do much cleaning of the cat's litter box.

Shawn Messonnier, D.V.M
Paws & Claws Animal Hospital
Plano, Texas
As the owner of a cat and a dog, you will need to get in a routine of visiting the vet, as well as taking care of your pets' health at home. Messonnier added that being able to afford proper care for both pets, practicing

preventive medicine for both pets, and knowing what you are getting into ahead of time will make these visits to the vet go smoothly. He also knows that while you have a new puppy in the home the cat could become very stressed out. Messonnier recommended pheromones, herbs, or volatile oils to calm down mild anxiety in a cat while it is going through the transition.

According to Messonnier, many pet owners are surprised to learn that cats and dogs do not need annual vaccinations. While it is important to give your pets the best medical attention for proper health, pets do not need to be vaccinated every year but rather when their antibody levels are low. There are specific vaccinations that go on yearly such as rabies and others for other specific times if there are diseases floating around your area. Messonnier also reminded owners that cats and dogs need their teeth cleaned. Their teeth get just as dirty as humans' teeth, and properly cleaning them to be sure of good oral care is essential.

CHAPTER 9

House-training Your Puppy

House-training your puppy is a very big step in the training and growth of your new companion. It may seem like a monumental task with many obstacles, but it is one that you can start as soon as the puppy joins the family. A dog matures very quickly compared with a human child. Four months of canine time is equivalent to four years of a child's life. Consider this when you are house-training your puppy, because human toddlers do not begin to be potty trained until 2 years old, and the average child is not fully potty trained until 4 years of age. The average puppy is house-trained by 4 months of age, but remember each is an individual and learns at different rates. You have the tools here to start this process the day you bring your new puppy home. You must prepare the home, the crate, and the outdoor space for waste elimination and you are ready to begin.

Preparing the Environment

When preparing your puppy's environment, first gather the materials that you will need to house-train your puppy. Have a collar and leash to be able to take it outside. A long leash, about 20 feet, allows the puppy to explore the elimination spot but still gives you control if it starts to stray. Have a roll of paper towels and odor neutralizer on hand to make cleanups fast and easy. A covered trash can keeps cleanup odors at a minimum. Prepare an easy pair of shoes to slip on and a jacket near the doorway. A towel will also be useful to wipe off wet or muddy paws when returning inside. You will also want to have your chosen crate assembled and ready, and baby gates to safely block off areas that you do not want your puppy to reach.

Crating Your Puppy

Crates are rectangular cages made of sturdy wire, molded plastic, canvas, or soft-sided strong fabric. Molded plastic crates are very strong and easy to clean. They are held together by nuts and bolts, and come in a variety of colors. They are usually the least expensive way to maintain your dog's sleeping environment, and most are suitable for airline travel requirements. Wire crates provide a good 360-degree view of the environment, often have two doors for easy access, and can fold flat. Canvas crates are lightweight and can be folded easily for travel. Soft-sided crates are lightweight and are appropriate for small and toy-size breeds. They are best suited for travel, may have a shoulder strap or wheels, and can be suitable for carry-on luggage on the airlines. The crate should be large enough for your dog to stand up and turn around, but not so large that it may want to eliminate waste at one end and sleep in the other.

Choose a crate that your puppy can grow into. You may have to block off some of the interior if it is too large to begin with, and remove the barrier as your puppy grows. Many different styles of crates are available, and they should be portable so you can travel with your dog's den. No matter where you go, it will always know where the safe spot is.

Choose one spot to place the crate; this will become your dog's home base. Because dogs are instinctually pack animals, they need to feel a part of the activity and be able to visualize the other family members. Place the crate in an area that is not isolated from daily activities. The living room may be a good place for this. A puppy that is isolated in another part of the house will often seek attention through excessive barking or trying to escape to be with its "pack." Your puppy will be integrated into the family much faster if it can see, observe, hear, and smell all the day's experiences.

The crate space provides not only your puppy a safety zone, but also your home. If you must leave the house for a period of time, you can securely put your puppy there and know there will be no chewing or destruction in your home. When you travel, the crate can be transported with you to new places, such as hotels or other friends' homes, and it gives the puppy a consistent familiar space. When you are home and able to supervise the puppy, let it out with the family to participate in daily events and play. The crate

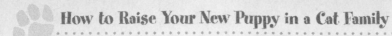
is a tool and not a convenience factor for inadequate supervision. Keep the crate door open when your puppy is out of the crate so it always has access to the safety zone and resting place. You will find that your dog actually seeks the crate out when it wants to take a nap or even go into to it to play with toys.

Anxious, shy, or unsure dogs need this den to feel safe from the world, or to retreat to when they are unsure of the situation at hand. If you are introducing a puppy to a crate for the first time after it has been used to a life of "freedom without borders," you may experience some resistance to the idea. But fear not, stay true to your belief that the den is a good space, and do not give in to the barking or whining that may ensue. This too, shall come to pass, and most puppies adapt to their crate within days. If you do not think the crate is a place you will want your dog sleeping all of its life, that is all right, but remember it will give you better control of the environment and your puppy during the house-training process.

Using the crate will help speed up the process of house-training because a dog does not wish to eliminate where it sleeps or eats. This is good news for you and enforces a place of safety, security, and cleanliness, and not a site to eliminate in. Adult dogs may be crated up to eight hours without accidents, but ideally would be allowed out to exercise and play. Young puppies who are 6 to 8 weeks old need to go out every one to two hours.

Fencing

Outdoor fencing is critical if you live in a busy neighborhood or if your pet has a tendency to wander. Many different fencing supplies are available, ranging from wooden privacy fence to mesh wire. The fence identifies an obvious boundary for waste elimination and protects your pet from escape or danger. Underground fencing is also available. The dog wears a collar that emits a warning or a shock when the dog approaches the fence boundary. Invisible Fence and PetSafe Boundary Control System are two manufacturers of these fencing systems. Regardless of the size of your dog's yard, always keep it clean and pick up fecal matter. This prevents contamination of children who may play there, odor and pest control, and curbs avoidance behavior when an area is soiled.

Cleanliness Deters Elimination

The home, sleeping, and outdoor environments should be kept as clean as possible to deter dogs from choosing misplaced areas to eliminate. The crate should be kept dry and clean and blankets laundered to prevent repeated elimination in the crate and to prevent bacterial infections on your dog's skin. Outdoor feces should be picked up and disposed to prevent disease and parasite transmission. When you take your puppy on a walk, you should carry a plastic bag to pick up and remove any feces from the walkway, park, road, or neighbor's yard.

If your dog has an accident, clean it up immediately with an enzymatic odor neutralizer. When a dog urinates, it initially does not have much odor, but as it starts to degrade, the odor will worsen and become stronger. If you do not properly clean this area and eliminate the odor, it will be a strong trigger for your dog to urinate in this place again. Urine is composed of urea, and this begins to break down into the strong smell of ammonia. Further breakdown produces mercaptans, which creates a very foul odor. Mercaptans are the chemicals that give rotten cabbage and skunk spray its unique potency.

Dogs have a tremendous sense of smell and a special odor-amplifying organ, the vomeronasal organ. This gives dogs a sense of smell 100 times that of humans, and odors that are undetectable to us can be significant stimuli for a dog. Enzymatic cleaners are most effective at removing these odors. Enzymes break down, digest, and destroy odors, not just cover or mask them with another smell. There are many quality nontoxic enzymatic cleaning products on the market today such as Nature's Miracle, Simple Solution Stain and Odor Remover, Nilodor, Get Serious Pet Stain Remover, Nilotex, No Scents, and Housesaver. Try to clean the urine or fecal odor immediately after an accident occurs to prevent the smell from triggering another episode.

A Designated Elimination Spot

Now that you have established the appropriate environment for your puppy, you need to choose a designated elimination spot so your puppy will begin to learn where it is supposed to eliminate waste. If you take your puppy outside to its designated elimination spot and it does not go, put the puppy back into the crate for 15 minutes, then return outside to the elimination spot. Your puppy needs to learn that you take it to this spot for a good reason, and meandering around or playing is not allowed. Repeat these steps by taking your puppy on the leash to the elimination spot, and if it does not "do business," take the puppy back inside and into the crate. Do this in 15-minute intervals, and soon your dog will realize what is expected on these "potty breaks." As a good rule of thumb, always take your puppy outside to eliminate first thing in the morning, after each meal and drink of water, after exercise and play periods, after a nap, before bedtime, and anytime it starts sniffing for a place to go.

Eventually you will not want to always have to leash your puppy to escort it to the elimination site. You can start by giving your puppy a little more freedom by walking, off leash, to the site, and use your verbal cue. Gradually, over a week, walk with your dog off leash, but bring your leash just in case, and accompany your puppy to the spot. The next week, accompany your puppy three-quarters of the way to the area, and make sure your dog continues the rest of the way alone. The next week, walk only halfway toward the site, and the following week only a quarter of the way. Eventually, you will be able to let your dog outside and watch it eliminate waste from the door. This is only an option for those who have fenced yards or large pieces of property. Do not attempt this technique if you live in a busy city or apartment complex — keep your dog on a leash for protection from harm. Remember to always pick up the poop, and do not let more than two piles accumulate in the designated area. An elimination site soiled with feces may discourage your dog from going in that spot. If your dog goes to another area of the yard that you do not want it to, do not correct this because it may cause fear of eliminating outdoors. Instead, get the puppy to the proper site by calling its name and trotting over the site: "Sam, come Sam, come do your business!"

You want to encourage your puppy during this process and give lavish praise when it eliminates in the proper spot. Also make sure your body language conveys what you want, because your puppy will pick up on these cues. You will also want to incorporate reward-based training into the house-training process.

Reward-Based Training

Making the right thing easy and rewarded and the wrong thing difficult using correction is the basis for reward-based training. Reward training gives the dog association between doing something right and a positive reward associated with the action. Clicker training is also used to reward the right action. Prior training must be used for the dog to associate its positive actions with the clicking noise. Food reward training is also an immediate positive gratification for doing the right thing. One of the drawbacks to food or clicker training is that the item must always be with you when you reward the action, and that may not always be possible. Several training guides can give you more information on how to use these other reward techniques. When you correct your dog, all you will need to say is "no." Do not hit your dog with a rolled up newspaper or your hand, and do not rub a dog's nose in its excrement or abuse it physically. Only correct the action if you catch the dog in the act, and never punish for something after the fact. Because dogs live in the moment, they do not associate the punishment with something they did before or feel remorse for something that happened in the past, even if it was just a couple of minutes ago)

Your dog will start to naturally give you cues that it needs to go outside if you observe closely. Some puppies, after a couple of weeks, may start to go to the door and stand, sit, bark, or scratch at the door when they need to go. You can also teach your dog to signal with a bark or whine. Start by having your dog practice the come, sit, and stay commands to get its brain in the "learning" mode. Then, to teach the speak command, say "speak," hold a treat up, and gently tease the puppy until it makes even the smallest sound, then reward it immediately. You can work this up to a full-fledged bark.

When your dog knows the "speak" command, you can transfer this to association with the door. When you get ready to take your dog outside the next time, clip on the leash but do not open the door yet. Create motivation and excitement about going outdoors and say, "speak." At the first sign of even a whine or vocalization in anticipation, open the door and immediately praise, "Good boy, good speak!" The dog will soon make the connection that the bark results in the door opening. Once your dog has learned the speak command at the door, do not use treats anymore. Your petting and praise will be reward enough, and we do not want to teach it that going to the door is rewarded treats. This will result in a dog that runs and barks at the door every time it wants a treat! You can also use a bell for your dog to signal that it needs to go out. Hang a large bird bell or sleigh bell on a piece of string or ribbon and hang it from the handle of the door. When your dog wants to go out, first have it sit at the door and then lift a paw to touch the bell and say, "ring." As soon as the bell makes a sound, open the door and praise, "good boy, good ring!" Eventually your dog will lift a paw and touch the bell or ring it with its nose to signal the need to go outside.

It cannot be overstressed how valuable a tool praise is. It is not necessarily the words you are using, it is the tone of your voice and the body language you are exhibiting. If your friend has her arms crossed and a stern look on her face when you asked her if "something was wrong" and she said "no," would you believe her? Her words may have indicated that nothing is wrong, but her body language clearly spoke volumes about her true feelings. Your dog is a very astute reader of body language, posture, and listening. Make sure that your body posture is relaxed, that you are not staring the dog down, and that you speak in a clear, soothing, encouraging tone. It is not suggested to use the dog's name when reprimanding or correcting the action of your dog because this may associate its name with a negative outcome. Any method of correction that occurs after the fact will only make it more difficult to train your dog, and may result in a dog that is fearful or afraid to eliminate in front of you. Be vigilant about supervising your dog both indoors and outdoors, allowing you to praise or correct the behavior in an immediate manner.

The Potty Picture

Now that you have a designated area picked out and have established reward-based training, it is time to talk about the big subject. Some people just do not want to talk about this subject. The subject of elimination. Some people are grossed out or just plain uncomfortable talking about bodily functions. But, this is one of the most common questions veterinarians ask about pets. "Are there any changes in drinking or urination? How do the feces look? Is there any diarrhea or vomiting?" These are such important components of overall health that veterinarians often look to these symptoms as indicators of a problem or disease. So, with that said, do not be embarrassed to inspect it, notice it, know how much, how often, and what it looks like — your puppy and veterinarian will be grateful that you know the answers to these awkward questions.

When you know what your puppy's urination and fecal patterns look like, you are inspecting for general health and well-being. It can tell you whether everything appears all right, or if there is reason for concern, what your dog is eating, and how it is digesting. Normal urination is light yellow in color and is a steady stream that lasts a few seconds, then stops. Females and young male dogs usually squat to urinate, and older males may lift their leg when urinating. Normal feces are formed well, light brown in color, often segmented, and should be expelled with little effort. Changes in these patterns can be an important indicator of a problem, and this will significantly affect house-training efforts.

Keep an eye out for abnormal patterns and what they could

mean. Stranguria, straining to urinate, is common with urinary tract infections, partial blockages, blood in urine, bladder tumors, or discomfort when urinating. The dog may initially look like it is urinating normally, but then stays in the squat position with only small drips of urine. The dog may walk on and quickly squat again and attempt to urinate. The dog may feel the sensation to urinate even though its bladder may be empty. It may also exhibit urine dripping or dribbling, or excessive licking.

Tenesmus, or straining to defecate, is common when a dog is having diarrhea or constipation or trying to pass a foreign object. A veterinary associate once saw a Labrador pass a whole Barbie doll! You just never know what is coming out unless you look. The dog may have to defecate more often, or feel like it is never quite finished, or may walk as it is attempting to defecate. The volume of feces passed may be copious or scant, have a very foul odor, or even blood in the feces.

Steatorrhea, or oily feces, leaves a glistening oily residue or rancid odor, which can indicate maldigestion of fats, often due to a pancreatic enzyme deficiency. Excess gas, or borborygmus, can indicate digestive upset and bloating or an overactive intestinal tract. Observe the feces for signs of foreign bodies such as plastic, aluminum foil, bone fragments, fiber, or other things that you may not have known that your puppy ate. If you observe any of these abnormal behaviors or eliminations, let your veterinarian know so that the problem can be fixed. Save a fresh sample of the stool or the urine if you can, or put it in the fridge overnight, so the vet can test the feces or urine for any problems.

The Behavior of Elimination

Dogs communicate through olfactory, visual, and vocal cues to other dogs. Dogs use their body language to communicate visually to other dogs. At 8 to 10 weeks old, a puppy must eliminate every hour. By 4 months of age, the puppy needs to go seven to eight times per day, and an adult dog goes three to five times per day. Puppies reach sexual maturity by 4 to 6 months of age, and all puppies should be house-trained by 6 months of age. Small-breed dogs mature faster than large-breed dogs, and certain breeds can be harder to train. Male puppies tend to take longer than females to house-train due to their tendency toward marking behavior. You can begin to read and anticipate a dog's body language and posture before a dog eliminates.

The sense of smell

The sense of smell in a dog is one of the most remarkable physical qualities of the canine species. A dog's nose is the equivalent to our fingerprint with a pattern of ridges and dimples that give a unique print to each dog. As a dog ages, often it will lose its sense of hearing or sight, but its sense of smell usually remains for a lifetime. Humans see the world first through vision; dogs, on the other hand, use smell as their first observation of the world and to make sense of what they hear and see. The result is an animal that "sees" via its nose rather than its eyes. Dogs have a specialized vomeronasal organ (VNO) in the roof of their mouth that allows them to detect and intensify the smell of pheromones that are vital to maternal care and sexual behavior. Dogs will flick their tongue in and out, as if drinking, to intensify a smell and gather it with the

VNO. A dog's sense of smell is 1,000 to 100,000 times stronger than a human's. Human noses have 6 million sensory receptor sites in their nasal passages, but dogs have up to 300 million. This allows a dog to detect a teaspoon of sugar dissolved in a million gallons of water, or two Olympic size swimming pools. A dog can detect human scent on a glass slide that has been lightly fingerprinted and left outside for two weeks. Dogs trained in arson detection can sniff out drops of lighter fluid or lamp oil in an environment covered in several inches of water, snow, mud, or fire debris.

Most dogs begin with an intense focused sniffing of the area before they eliminate. They smell for the presence of another dog, urine, or the smell of feces and other odors. A dog postures in a squatting position before urinating. Prior to defecating, a dog may travel to a more distant space and begin circling, and then squat with the hind end and spine curved down. By observing these subtle behaviors, you will be able to correct or redirect the activity to a more desirable area. All puppies should be allowed to eliminate immediately upon exiting the crate, after eating or playing, and upon waking.

Maintain your posture

Your own body posture also communicates a great deal to a dog. Your presence in a relaxed, calm, non-staring, non-intimidating way will help your dog complete its "duty" outside, while still allowing you to observe and praise the action. If a dog senses tension, anger, or intimidating behaviors from its owner, it may become afraid to eliminate in front of you. If dogs sense extreme fear, stress, or anxiety, they may urinate, defecate, or express their anal glands. Submissive urination may occur if a dog is trying to communicate its submission to another dog or human, and may be associated with a reprimand or upon excitement. This behavior is more common in young female puppies, and most puppies will outgrow this behavior by the time they are a year old. When accompanying your dog outside, assess your own posture and presence to encourage the correct behavior from your dog. Look for and read the signals that your puppy may show you when it needs to eliminate, often exhibited as going to the door, whining, acting restless, intense sniffing on the floor, or circling.

Other behaviors

To differentiate urine-marking behavior from simple urination, the place, surface, and circumstances will offer the answer. Urine marking is often deposited on vertical surfaces (a tree, the end of a couch, a wall) and involves small quantities of urine on the target. Sexually mature female dogs can also exhibit marking behavior. Limit a dog's exposure to stimuli that may trigger marking behavior, make the target aversive to the dog, and correct immediately when the behavior begins. Neutering male dogs and spaying female dogs will often completely eliminate this unwanted behavior.

Some Common Misconceptions

There are some important facts and misconceptions that you should be familiar with in knowing what and what not to expect from your puppy. This information will help alleviate some of the frustrations that may occur during this process. Animal behaviorist Jolanta Benal and author of *The Dog Trainer's Quick and Dirty Tips for Teaching and Caring for Your Pet*, describes some of the most common misconceptions that a pet owner may experience, and they are presented here in summary:

Overestimating capacity of the puppy

Many owners make the mistake of overestimating the "carrying" and "holding" capacity of their dog. Puppies are often able to sleep, up to eight hours, through the night, and owners often expect them to hold it during the day for long periods of time. Unfortunately, your puppy cannot physically "hold it" this long during the day. During the night there is very little to no "input" into the puppy — no food or water — and therefore there is no "output." Metabolism and the production of urine and feces is also slowed during sleep.

This is not the case during the day. A puppy will be eating and drinking during the daytime, and will therefore be producing waste material as its body metabolizes food into energy. An old rule of thumb used to estimate how long your dog can hold it is the number of hours equal to his age in months plus one. For example, an 8-week-old puppy could, in theory, hold its elimination for two months (eight weeks) plus one, which equals three hours.

Some estimates are more conservative, such as information from the San Francisco Society for the Prevention of Cruelty to Animals (SFSPCA), which provides a house-training tip sheet that states the maximum time for a 4-month-old puppy is only three hours. It is better for a pet owner to always err on the side of caution to avoid accidents by allowing more elimination breaks. The muscles of young dogs and young humans are not fully developed, and therefore they are not able to hold their bowels or urine for very long periods of time.

How many potty breaks are enough?

New dog owners of puppies or older dogs should expect to take their dog out frequently at first. This will help you more quickly get to know your dog's elimination habits. The newborn puppy eliminates every hour when awake. Each week thereafter, you can add another 30 minutes to the time that it is able to "hold it." The very young puppy should be allowed to eliminate outside, then given only a few minutes of freedom in the room before going back into the crate until the next potty break. This is a good way to prevent accidents in the room, and teaches the puppy to not eliminate in the resting area. This also helps in the development of the muscles that enable the puppy to control waste elimination.

Some owners may think that once a puppy has eliminated, it will not need to go again until the next scheduled time. This is not always the case, and it is important to observe your puppy for signs and signals that indicate the need to eliminate again. The three most frequent signs of this behavior are restlessness, circling, and intently sniffing the ground. Puppies will also usually eliminate within 15 minutes of eating or drinking and immediately upon waking up. Any activity, such as playing or chewing, will also stimulate elimination, so be sure to take your puppy outside after these activities, too.

Walking the trainee

Many people who have the time enjoy walking their puppy through the neighborhood or the park. Although walking your dog is a very healthy habit for both you and your dog, it can work against the house-training process if you are not careful. Before you start a walk, the puppy should be allowed to eliminate and be praised dearly for doing so. Take the puppy on a leash to the elimination site and just stand there. Do not do anything except wait two to three minutes for the puppy to eliminate. As soon as it does, praise it immediately. If the puppy does not go, take it back inside and into the crate, wait 10 to 15 minutes, and go outside to the site again. After waste elimination, it is time to walk as a reward. Prompt elimination is what you want to see happen. Dogs that are taken immediately on a walk are often distracted or overwhelmed with other sights and scents and they may not eliminate. These dogs may also associate that when they are walked and then they do eliminate, they are immediately taken back home and into their crate. These dogs may start to intentionally hold it, just so they can remain outdoors longer. This may lead to a dog that then, when returning to the house, drops the "load" in the house as soon as it comes in the door. Use the walk as the reward, not as the elimination time.

When Accidents Happen

Despite all your best efforts, accidents will happen. These are teaching opportunities for you and not the puppy. Here are some things to think about and troubleshoot what went wrong.

Evaluate your timing. Were you watching your puppy closely or was it out of your immediate sight? How about your body posture and language? Did you look intimidating, act angry, speak loudly, shout, or cause excessive excitement to your puppy? If you did not catch the dog in the act, do not punish it. It cannot relate its natural behavior to a time in the past that made you mad. You must catch the puppy in the act to correct it.

If your puppy has eliminated in its crate, reevaluate the crate space. Is it too big, so the puppy can relieve itself in one end and sleep in the other? Is it clean and odor-free so it does not stimulate the behavior? Did you put papers in the crate or feed and water your puppy in the crate and not take it outside in a timely manner? How long was your puppy in the crate, and was it allowed to eliminate waste outside? How old is your puppy, and can it really "hold it" that long? If your puppy had an accident in another part

of the home, it may not necessarily recognize this space as inside space, especially if it is not a room the puppy is familiar with. Introduce your puppy slowly and repetitively to more spaces in the house and interact with it so it soon recognizes it as an inside space in which not to eliminate.

Odors are a significant stimulus for dogs and can persist in the environment for a long time. Did you properly clean, and not just mask, prior odors in the carpet or bedding? Was the site of elimination an area that was previously marked by either your dog or another? Did you properly choose a designated area to eliminate in or does the puppy have free roam of its environment? If you have used all the proper odor removal steps and your dog still keeps eliminating on this spot, you may try feeding your dog at this site to discourage this behavior. Because a dog does not like to eliminate where it eats, this technique uses natural behavior to your benefit to modify the problem. Continue feeding your dog at least a week at this spot before reverting to the original feeding spot. If the problem reoccurs, repeat feeding at this spot. Adult dogs that have a long history of this inappropriate elimination may take up to six weeks to retrain.

Distractions abound for puppies as they are exploring a new environment and think "the world is their oyster." Were there interruptions to the schedule, or new people or pets in the household? Was there a lot of excitement and play occurring? Was the puppy preoccupied the last time it was outside and did not eliminate? It takes focus for a puppy to know when and where it needs to go to relieve itself, and puppies are easily distracted by these other factors. Remember to lead your puppy to the site, give your cue, and do not dance around the subject. It should eliminate within five minutes of being taken to the spot. Try not to confuse your puppy by initiating play or any other activity until it has eliminated waste.

If your dog has marked on your bed, clothing, armchair, the baby's toys, another dog's bed, or even you, your dog is most likely trying to establish dominance over you and your (and in the puppy's mind, its) things. This is unacceptable behavior, and neutering will likely stop this from continuing. Further training and leadership exercises will establish your role as pack leader and earn respect from your dog.

When you take your puppy to a new or unfamiliar place, it may not recognize it as you do as an "off-limit" zone for elimination. The puppy may recognize that it is not correct to eliminate in its home space, but this is not the home space. To avoid these mistakes in your neighbor's home or a place of business, make sure to give your puppy ample opportunity to eliminate outdoors before entering a new place. You must teach it that eliminating in any indoor place, not just the home, is wrong.

Medical conditions leading to accidents

If you have gone through your checklist and cannot find any human error as a possible cause for the accident occurring, then your dog may have a medical or behavioral condition. The behavioral conditions that can cause house soiling are anxiety-related elimination, excitement and submissive urination, urine marking, or cognitive dysfunction syndrome.

Dogs with anxiety-related elimination show this behavior when

they experience extreme fear or surprise or are separated from their owners. This behavior is often accompanied by other signs of stress such as excessive panting, pacing, vocalization, destruction, or escape behavior. They may express their anal glands, urinate, or defecate.

Submissive urination usually occurs in young dogs. It occurs as a signal of submission to other dogs or humans. The puppy will often have its ears back, avoid eye contact, cower, or roll over. Puppies may dribble or squirt small amounts of urine. Most puppies outgrow this behavior by about 7 months of age, but it can occur at any age. To minimize this behavior, owners and other people should greet the puppy in a less-threatening manner by kneeling down, averting their eyes, and petting under the chest and not over the head. When arriving home, do not greet or make eye contact with your dog immediately, wait at least five minutes and let your dog settle down. Crouch down to your dog's level to approach and pet it, do not bend over. Guests should not greet the dog, and should sit down. They should not approach the dog. As the dog approaches them, they should speak softly and not make eye contact. Avoid any reprimands or harsh tone in your voice. As puppies grow, most will develop more confidence and outgrow these conditions. You should never punish your puppy for submissive urination, because this may only worsen the problem. You can engage the puppy in another activity, such as tossing a ball or commanding it to sit, to divert this behavior.

Urine marking can occur even when adequate opportunity has been given to the dog for urination. The dog often lifts its leg and urine is deposited in small quantities, usually on a vertical surface. Some female dogs also mark in the squatting position. Marking behavior may start at 3 months of age. Marking territory outside is a dog's way of indicating to other members its territory and dominance within the pack and acts like a "calling card" to others. This behavior is common in unaltered male dogs and is often triggered by a female dog in estrus, another dog or pet, or a new item or person in the household. This behavior often begins with the onset of sexual maturity at 6 to 24 months. This is not a house-training problem, but a behavioral problem. Dogs that are urine marking are trying to establish their dominance over a territory. These dogs may exhibit this behavior due to the presence of another male urine odor, the presence of females in estrus, jealousy over a new pet or baby, a visitor in the house, or when they feel anxious or nervous about a new situation and want to express their dominance. Neutering a male dog, making the targets averse, and limiting a dog's exposure to these stimuli will help curtail this behavior. Allowing your dog more exercise and outside time will give these dogs ample opportunity to mark outdoors rather than indoors. Neutering your pet before the onset of sexual maturity by 6 months of age will help eliminate this behavior before it becomes a habit.

Cognitive dysfunction syndrome as a cause of house soiling occurs in elderly dogs usually older than 7 years of age. This is a form of canine senility, and dogs may "forget" to ask to go outside and eliminate in the house, even though they were previously house-trained. This behavior is often accompanied by other signs such as getting lost in the house, changes in social behavior, disorientation, vocalization, and changes in sleep and wake cycles.

Urinary tract infections or puppy vaginitis may cause a sense of urgency and frequent urination. Parasites can cause diarrhea or constipation and vomiting. Sudden dietary changes or the addition of a new food or treat may trigger diarrhea and frequent soft, loose stool that moves more quickly through the digestive tract. Bacteria, viruses, and inflammatory bowel disease (IBD) may also cause an urgent, frequent diarrhea. Females in estrus, usually first observed at 6 to 8 months of age, often urinate more frequently. Sexually mature male dogs, at 6 to 24 months old, may start exhibiting territorial marking behavior, usually on vertical surfaces. Neutering can help deter most of this behavior. Toxins, such as antifreeze, that have been ingested may cause vomiting and diarrhea and urination. Hormonal or age-influenced incontinence may develop and cause urine leakage, especially when the dog is at rest. Some congenital diseases, such as bladder wall defects, can also cause more frequent, sporadic urination. Excess drinking (polydipsia) and resultant excess urination (polyuria) are side effects of other medical conditions such as Cushing's disease or kidney dysfunction. Closely observe how often and how much your puppy is drinking and eliminating and for any signs of vomiting or dehydration. You can also collect a urine or fecal sample for your veterinarian to evaluate. Arthritis, pain, cognitive dysfunction syndrome (CDS), or senility in older dogs can be a cause of house soiling. Separation anxiety can often cause a dog to eliminate when the owner is absent. Contact your veterinarian for an appointment to rule out any underlying condition that could be affecting the success of your puppy's house-training.

Marking behavior is one of the biggest frustrations owners face and often is one of the most common behavioral problems that owners encounter. Marking territory is a natural pack behavior that signals to others their presence, sexual maturity, territory, and dominance. At least 60 percent of male dogs will stop marking behavior within weeks to months after getting neutered, and virtually all females will stop marking behavior after spaying, according to Dr. Nicholas Dodman of Tufts University. Neutering your pet also prevents roaming and causes less aggressive behavior. Spaying or neutering your dog is best done before 6 months of age, when sexual maturity is reached. The longer you wait, the more likely the marking behavior will become a habit for your dog and more difficult to break.

Coprophagia, or the ingestion of feces, is a very disturbing behavior a dog may exhibit. It is hard to want to lavish those "puppy kisses" when your dog has just eaten fecal matter. Young dogs are more likely to engage in this behavior, especially when they are "testing" their environment with their mouths, but it can occur at any age. Dogs may eat their own feces or the feces of other dogs or animals. Different theories exist as to why dog eat feces, and include exploring their environment, establishing intestinal microflora (beneficial bacteria and microbes), boredom, scent removal, or compensating for a nutritional deficiency. Mother dogs routinely eat the feces of their puppies up until 3 to 4 weeks of age until the puppy learns to eliminate outside the den space. This is a defensive technique the mother uses to maintain hygiene within the den, but also to remove any odors that may attract predators. Rule out a nutritional or pancreatic deficiency and consider diet change to alter the stool. Provide your dog with adequate exercise

and play to prevent boredom. You can apply an adverse "taste" to the feces by applying hot sauce or add a substance like FOR-BID (monosodium glutamate) to food to make the taste of the feces aversive. Always try to pick up feces soon after it is deposited to keep your yard sanitary and to avoid temptation for your dog to find and eat the feces.

When frustration does occur, and it will, remember you are teaching a new skill and it will not be automatic until your puppy practices it many, many times. When you find yourself overwhelmed with frustration or anger or wanting to become abusive, stop what you are doing, step away, take some deep breaths, give yourself or your puppy a "time out," give yourself some laughter, and freely give forgiveness to your puppy.

Punishing mistakes

People often react adversely and emotionally to a dog's accident or mistake in the house. Although it is very frustrating, the act of punishing a dog for these mistakes is a major pitfall to the success of your house-training technique. Never punish any behavior that occurred more than just a few seconds ago. Your dog will not make the association between your anger and the act if it is corrected after the fact. If you scold your puppy in the act of peeing on the new wool rug, it does not understand that you are angry for peeing on the nice rug. The puppy is only going to associate big, scary, mad you when eliminating in front of you. This may lead to a puppy that will not eliminate in front of you, even if you want it to outside. Your puppy may become fearful and anxious as it becomes nervous about eliminating any time you are looking. Some trainers suggest an interruption technique such as a "chhhh" sound, a noisemaker, a sharp "no," or even a clap. For the more sensitive pup, a more gentle distraction may be all that is necessary to interrupt the behavior. The noise should be loud enough to interrupt but not scare or cause fear in the puppy. If you stick to a schedule and observe closely for the behavior before elimination occurs, you will seldom need to use these distraction techniques.

Distraction techniques

You may not be 100 percent effective at getting your puppy to the proper elimination spot every time, but you can interrupt the behavior until you can get it there. If you catch your puppy "in the act," immediately interrupt the behavior with a distraction. Your voice is the simplest, fastest correction you can make, and you should say "no, no, no" and promptly take your puppy outside, then say the trigger phase and provide a reward if it finishes eliminating outside. Whatever word you choose should be sharp and definite in your tone and relay disapproval. Another distraction tool is noisemakers, such as pennies in a can that you shake when your puppy is behaving inappropriately. Remember, these are not punishments but are distractions to reset your puppy's mind away from the behavior that it is engaging in.

Waste-Elimination Alternatives

There are other alternatives to eliminating outdoors. You may want an indoor alternative if you live in the city or an apartment, are elderly or handicapped, have a small dog, travel, own a young puppy who does not have good muscle control of its bladder or bowels, or have a geriatric dog that cannot hold its urine or has trouble getting outdoors. The other options you may then consider are paper or a potty pad, or litter pan training. House-training and paper training are two different practices and each has its own rules and requirements.

House-training is teaching the dog that it is never appropriate to eliminate indoors, while paper training encourages indoor elimination. Paper training is not used to teach outdoor elimination. Paper training is an aid for eliminating indoors that you can clean up easily and is best suited for toy- and small-breed dogs, or for city dwellers that may not have regular access to an outdoor area. Potty pads are moisture-proof pads that have a plastic sheet backing that protects surfaces. Like the outdoor designated area, the pad can also become a more defined space for elimination. Take the puppy to the pad and use your trigger phrase. You may also encourage elimination on the pad by placing some prior urine or fecal odor on the pad. This will strongly signify that this is a spot to eliminate on. Newspapers should be stacked at least ten sheets thick placed over a plastic bag that is cut open and laid out to prevent urine from soaking through. Litter pans can be lined with paper and are another elimination option for toy-breed dogs. You may also use the pad in the crate when your puppy is very young or you have to leave it for longer periods of time that may necessitate waste elimination; however, try to avoid this because you do not want to encourage this behavior in the crate. Use the same technique when training on paper as you would outdoors: lead your puppy to the site, use your trigger phrase to initiate elimination, and praise. Always remember to keep the elimination site away from the food, water, and sleeping area.

If your puppy was raised in a "puppy mill," it was likely not allowed outside of the kennel or crate very often if at all. As a result, the puppy was forced to eliminate and soil where it slept. Puppies that were removed too early from their mother also do not learn to be clean and may learn to soil where they sleep. These circumstances may make your puppy more difficult to train using the crate. In these cases, you may consider other options such as an exercise pen, a safe room with baby gates, litter pans, or even a box of sod so the puppy can learn to eliminate in these new areas rather than in its sleeping space.

CHAPTER
10

Tips for a Troubled Pair

If you are finding that no matter what you do, all of the strategies you learned are not working, you may be frustrated and wonder if something is wrong with you or your pets. This book gave you insights on the individual habits of cats and dogs and everything you can do to prepare ahead of time and start training them from the start; however, you may encounter more than just pet rivalry and first-time awkwardness between your cat and new puppy that you were not expecting. Your pets may experience anxiety and fear each other. This could be because of one or both of the pets, as well as your home situation and how that can affect the animals.

When this happens, many pet owners choose to give a pet away.

This may be the ultimate solution for serious aggression problems, but in most cases, it is just the easy way out. People would rather get rid of a problem than solve it, and if it makes life easier for them, they could find another home for the dog or cat. This concept was brought up early on to prove a point: It is not impossible for a cat and a dog to learn to get along, and the purpose of this book was to set the stage to show you how it can work.

However, you might have a pet that turned out to be unsuitable, and finding a new home for it might be better. Some animals have very specific needs and having another pet in the house is just unacceptable, but truly this is rare and is more common in cats and dogs with severe behavior problems. There are lots of places you can go to get help with finding out what is making your cat and dog unable to live in the same house. Try contacting a professional animal behaviorist or your veterinarian. There are also pet consultants available to help you solve your pet dilemmas.

If you decide you need to find a new home for a pet, there are several options. Placing classifieds in newspapers will reach a large audience. You can also place free advertisements online on Craigslist or on social media sites such as Facebook. Take caution when posting advertisements online and in newspapers. Do not include too much personal information, such as your home address. If possible, arrange to meet potential buyers at a public location, rather than inviting them into your home. It is wise to question potential buyers about their intentions and capabilities to raise a pet — you do not want Cruella De Vil adopting your dog or cat. If you purchased your dog from a breeder, consult your contract first. It is likely one term of the contract is that the dog is to be returned to the breeder in the event you cannot take care of it.

Getting Professional Help

There are many different sources of professional help to aid you in training your dog or discovering if your pet has a behavioral problem that needs attention. You can start your search for help with your veterinarian or local pet stores. Many either hold classes or at least have staff members that know many local trainers. There are also national organizations that can provide you with help and can often refer you to local help. Among these groups are nationwide organizations such as the International Association of Animal Behavior Consultants (IAABC), whose website is **www .iaabc.org**. There is a locator on the site that allows viewers to enter their location and find a consultant that is local, as well as information on conferences and organization events.

Another is the Association of Pet Dog Trainers (APDT), which can be found online at **www.apdt.com**. They specialize in dog training and gaining obedience from your puppy. Its website also has a search for local areas for prospective clients, as well as plenty of information for the web reader and providing many options and ideas.

What Went Wrong?

Do not automatically think of yourself as a bad owner if your cat and puppy are fighting and causing problems. You may have not

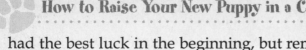

had the best luck in the beginning, but remember that it does not mean it is too late. Even if the puppy has grown up, your job is not done. You must enforce the same discipline and rules you did when it was young.

It is common for many pet owners to believe they are enforcing the right training, but in reality they have been doing it wrong from the start. Keeping the animals separated too much comes with another common problem: forcing them to interact too much. When pet owners force their animals together constantly, it makes the animals very uncomfortable as they are not in control of anything and are basically being thrown at a strange animal. It eliminates the curiosity and exhilarating mystery of getting to know a new friend and could result in them wanting nothing to do with each other. While on their own, if the pets are not playing together, pet owners take this as a bad sign. Is it really so bad that the animals can pass each other in the home without attacking? This is not a bad thing at all, but rather a sign that the pets respect each other. If they are not playing all the time, why is that a bad thing? Of course, you have the right thought to believe that your pets have their reasons if they are deliberately avoiding each other. Give them more supervised meetings and make sure you are present where you are close enough. They need to see you because they are looking for your approval and comfort. Practice having them meet and be in the same room together all over again while making sure neither one of them makes an intimidating move.

It is also comforting to know that cats and dogs are known to have the least amount of conflicts with one another. A different animal means a different situation, and it is not so much another pet that would be a threat but rather the fear of the unknown. If the cat and dog are getting in each other's way, they are most of the time small but cumbersome problems, like fighting over some food that was dropped on the floor. Tiny, frisky playthings grow older and bigger and become more of a threat to the cat. Before, the puppy was just a harmless dog that wanted to get into everything, but now it has matured and has grown to be much smarter. This is a mistake many pet owners make in letting the puppy play-attack the cat because it is just a puppy. They think that they should wait until the pup is older to start enforcing safety rules.

A major trouble cats and dogs face is that dogs often want to chase cats. Cats see this as a threat and may swat at a dog or run off into hiding as a form of self-defense. By using obedience training, your puppy will learn to listen to the owner and develop a sense of self-control when around your cat. Teach your puppy the command, "leave it!" when it starts to pester your cat. Because they are two entirely different species, it may be difficult for them to get along at first. Do not pressure them to be together. Gradually introduce your pets and let them establish a friendship on their own terms.

Weeks or months may pass before your cat and puppy can be trusted fully on their own. A year may even pass before they fully accept each other. Until then the two will need to be separated if you cannot supervise them. Even then, make sure your cat has a high perch where it can get away from your puppy. In time, the cat and puppy will likely grow to accept each other. Even if they only tolerate each other, they will at least not be left alone when you and other family members are not home.

Conclusion

Congratulations! You are the proud owner of not only a frisky feline but also an adorable new puppy. This book supplied you with the information to choose the best type of dog for your family and how to prepare your home and cat for its arrival. It also gave you methods for introducing your cat and puppy to each other, as well as training tips and details about the health of your pets. Some owners will have no problems getting their cat and dog to get along, while others may still be struggling with some lingering behavioral issues. If the latter is you, stay consistent and be persistent and you will succeed. You may need to hire some professional help, but as long as your pets are physically and mentally healthy, your hard work will pay off. There are many resources in the back of this book to help you continue your research. Do not give up just yet!

Although we are all different species, cats and dogs find ways to teach us something about them we never knew. There is a great mystery in trying to figure out what they are thinking, feeling, and how they really see the world around them. They also teach us about ourselves, as we can be ourselves around our pets without fear of judgment. Your pets could also help you live a longer and happier life. Take good care of them, and they will reward you with love and affection for as long as they live.

Whoever said you can't buy happiness forgot little puppies.
– Gene Hill, author

There are two means of refuge from the miseries of life: music and cats.
– Albert Schweitzer, philosopher

Resources

Cats

- Catster.com (**www.catster.com**) — A site for cat lovers for general information and entertainment. It also hosts a free copy of *The Cat Owner's Manual.*

- The Cat Fanciers' Association (**www.cfainc.org**) — Large registry of pedigree cats with information about showing, breeding, and caring for cats.

- Cats International (**www.catsinternational.org/index .html**) — Nonprofit educational organization providing information on cats.

Dogs

- Dogster (**www.dogster.com**) — A site for dog lovers. It also hosts a free copy of *The Dog Owner's Manual.*

- The American Kennel Club Association (**www.akc.org**) — Considered a standard in breeding.

- Dogs in Depth (**www.dogsindepth.com/index.html**) — An online dog encyclopedia.

- DogStarDaily (**www.dogstardaily.com**) — A comprehensive dog site, including their *Digital Dog Training Manual*.

- Bark Talk (**www.barktalk.com/breeders.html**) — Information on how to find a good breeder.

Pet Health

- Spay USA (**www.spayusa.org**) — A website that discusses everything you need to know about spaying and neutering, including locations you can get the surgery done for your pet.

- Pet Education (**www.peteducation.com**) — Doctors Foster and Smith's site; it lists health issues for all types of pets.

- American Animal Hospital Association (**www.healthypet .com**) — The "pet owners" site from the American Animal Hospital Association. Provides help finding a reputable animal hospital, as well numerous helpful articles in the Pet Care Library.

- The Pet Center (**www.thepetcenter.com**) — Provides accurate and easy-to-understand pet health care information. The Pet Center is partnered with National Pet Pharmacy to provide medical supplies.

- Mar Vista Animal Medical Center (**www.marvistavet.com/ index.html**) — Provides vaccine and health information.

- Pet Care Naturally (**www.petcarenaturally.com**) — Dr. Shawn's website on holistic pet care. Also offers organic pet care supplies.

Products

- Grannick's Bitter Apple (**www.bitterapple.com**) — A taste deterrent made by Grannick's for behavioral correction.

- Feliway (**www.feliway.com/us**) — Feline pheromones that help calm cats and correct behaviors.

- Kong (**www.kongcompany.com/worlds_best.html**) — Considered some of the toughest dog toys around, as well as the most fun.

- Greenies (**www.greenies.com**) — Treats for cats and dogs that help keep their teeth clean.

Behavior & Training

- Karen Pryor Clicker Training (**www.clickertraining.com**) — Karen Pryor's clicker training website. All your clicker needs are here.

- International Association of Animal Behavior Consultants (**www.iaabc.org**) — Find an animal behavior consultant near you.

- Association of Pet Dog Trainers (**www.apdt.com**) — Association for dog trainers.

- K9 Aggression (**www.k9aggression.com**) — A website that provides help for owners of aggressive dogs.

- Perfect Paws (**www.perfectpaws.com**) — A website that provides training information about cats and dogs.

Adoption & Pet Well-Being Organizations

- Alley Cat Allies (**www.alleycat.org**) — An organization that helps improve the lives of feral cats.

- Emergency Animal Rescue (**www.emergencyanimal rescue.org**) — An organization that rescues animals in life-threatening situations.

- The Dumb Friends League (**www.ddfl.org**) — "Dumb" references the inability to speak in this case. They provide adoption services to the Rocky Mountain region, as well as investigate animal cruelty cases and offer public animal education.

- Pet Finder (**www.petfinder.com**) — Pet adoption search engine for all of the U.S. Includes much more that just cats and dogs. Unfortunately, you must beware of backyard breeders posting here. Also hosts information on pet care, health, and training.

Bibliography

Becker, Marty, D.V.M., Mikkel Becker, Carol Kline, Gina Spadafori. *The Ultimate Cat Lover*. Health Communications, Inc.: Deerfield Beach, FL. 2008

Bonham, Margaret H. *The Cat Owner's Problem Solver: How to Manage Common Behavior Problems by Thinking Like your Cat*. T.F.H. Publications, Inc.: Neptune City, NJ. 2008

Dr. Brunner, David, Sam Stall. *The Cat Owner's Manual*. Quirk Books: Philadelphia, PA. 2004

Dr. Brunner, David, Sam Stall. *The Dog Owner's Manual*. Quirk Books: Philadelphia, PA. 2004

Church, Christine. *How to Keep Your Indoor Cat Sane and Sound*. Howell Book House and Wiley Publishing, Inc.: Hoboken, NJ. 2005.

Crute, Sheree, Susan Easterly, Tony Farrell, Susan McCullough,

Christian Millman, Jana Murphy, Amy D. Shojai. *The Well-Mannered Dog*. Rodale Press, Inc: Emmaus, PA. 1999

Moore, Arden. *The Cat Behavior Answer Book: Practical Insights & Proven Solutions for Your Feline Questions*. Storey Publishing: North Adams, MA. 2007

Moore, Arden. *The Dog Behavior Answer Book: Practical Insights & Proven Solutions for Your Canine Questions*. Storey Publishing: North Adams, MA. 2006

Welton, Roger L. D.V.M., *Canine and Feline 101: A Complete Guide for Selecting, Training, and Caring for Dogs and Cats*. iUniverse: Lincoln, NE. 2005

"Polluted Pets: Chemical exposures and pets' health." Environmental Working Group. **www.ewg.org/node/26239**.

Research Websites

Cat training and intelligence:

Lancaster, J. Justin. "Sasha, The Cat Who Used Tools." About. com. **http://cats.about.com/od/behaviortraining/a/cattools.htm**.

"Cat Clicker Training." Love to Know Cats. **http://cats.loveto know.com/Cat_Clicker_Training**.

Dog training and intelligence:

"Training Your Puppy to Live with the Cat." PupListings.com. **www.puplistings.com/dog-articles/training-puppy-to-live -with-cat.html**.

"Dogs: Positive Reinforcement Training." The Humane Sociaety of the United States. **www.humanesociety.org/animals/dogs/tips/dog_training_positive_reinforcement.html**.

Pet Education.com. **www.peteducation.com**.

Advice on how to introduce a puppy to a cat:

Moore, Cindy. "Behavior: Understanding and Modifying." K9 Web. **www.k9web.com/dog-faqs/behavior.html**.

American Psychological Association. **www.apa.org/releases/dogs-think.html**.

"Crate Training." American Dog Trainers Network. **www.inch.com/~dogs/cratetraining.html**.

"Crate Training." The Humane Society of the United States. **www.humanesociety.org/animals/dogs/tips/crate_training.html**.

"Teaching Your Dog to Stay." Washington Area Humane Society. **www.washingtonpashelter.org/PDF/Stay.pdf**.

"Confinement and Crate Training." The San Diego Humane Society. **www.sdhumane.org/site/DocServer/BT_K9-Crate_Training.pdf?docID=571**.

"Letting Your Dog Sleep on Your Bed." Professor's House. **www.professorshouse.com/pets/dogs/letting-your-dog-sleep-on-your-bed.aspx**.

Cat health:

"How to Trim a Cat's Nails." eHow. **www.ehow.com/how_6484**

_trim-cats-nails.html.

"Cat Health: Not Eating." CatHealthIssues.net. **www.cathealth issues.net/cat-not-eating.html**.

Plotnick, Arnold. "Hair Loss in Cats." Manhattan Cat Specialists. **www.manhattancats.com/Articles/hair_loss_in_cats.html**.

The Cat Fancier's Association. **www.cfa.org/articles/health/ FeLV.html**.

The Cat Health Guide. **www.cat-health-guide.org**.

Medscape. **www.medscape.com**.

PetMD. **www.petmd.com**.

"What Does FVRCP Stand For?" Chatsworth Veterinary Center Virtual Library. **www.chatvet.com/fvrcp.htm**.

Dog health:
"Kennel Cough (Infectious Tracheobronchitis) in Dogs." PetEducation.com. **www.peteducation.com/article.cfm?c=2 +2102&aid=452**.

"Causes of Vaccine Failure: Why Vaccinated Dogs Still Get Sick." PetEducation.com. **www.peteducation.com/article.cfm?c=2 +1648&aid=966**.

"Benefits of Spay/Neuter for Cats and Dogs." Spay USA. **www .spayusa.org/main_directory/02-facts_and_education/benefits _sn.asp**.

"2006 AAHA Canine Vaccine Guidelines, Revised."

American Animal Hospital Association. **www.aahanet.org/ PublicDocuments/VaccineGuidelines06Revised.pdf**.

Butler, Joy. "Is Your Puppy Teething?" Suite101.com. **www.dog -training.suite101.com/article.cfm/is_your_puppy_teething -a35741**.

Spadafori, Gina. "Ask a Dog Breeder These Questions Before You Buy." VeterinaryPartner.com. **www.veterinarypartner.com/ Content.plx?P=A&A=302**.

Pet behavior:
Dumb Friend's League. **www.ddfl.org/behavior/pica.pdf**.

"Why Do Cats Purr?" Scientific American. **www.scientific american.com/article.cfm?id=why-do-cats-purr**.

Copley, Jennifer. "Purring Helps with Healing." Suite101.com. **www.cats.suite101.com/article.cfm/purring_helps_with _healing**.

"Woof! The truth behind common dog myths." MSNBC. **www .msnbc.msn.com/id/12079937**.

Mestel, Rosie. "Ascent of the Dog." Discover Magazine. **www .discovermagazine.com/1994/oct/ascentofthedog434**.

"Every Dog Needs a Den." American Humane Association. **www .americanhumane.org/protecting-animals/adoption-pet-care/ care/dog-dens.html**.

Pet Sitters International. **www.petsit.com**.

Body language:

"Talking Dog: Body Language." Stacy's Wag 'N' Train. **www
.wagntrain.com/BodyLanguage.htm**.

"How to Interpret Your Dog's Body Language, Facial
Expressions, and Vocalizations." Paws Across America. **www
.pawsacrossamerica.com/interpret.html**.

Pet emotions:

Firth, Shannon. "The Dark Side of Devotion: Your Dog May Be
Jealous." findingDulcinea.com. **www.findingdulcinea.com/
news/science/2009/march/Is-Your-Dog-Jealous.html**.

"What Really Prompts the Dog's 'Guilty Look.'" Science Daily.
www.sciencedaily.com/releases/2009/06/090611065839.htm.

"Basic emotions." Changing Minds. **www.changingminds.org/
explanations/emotions/basic%20emotions.htm**.

Statistics:

"HSUS Pet Overpopulation Estimates." The Humane Society of
the United States. **www.humanesociety.org/issues/pet_over
population/facts/overpopulation_estimates.html**.

"The Top Ten Reasons for Pet Relinquishment to Shelters in the
United States." National Council on Pet Population Study &
Policy. **www.petpopulation.org/topten.html**.

"Rabies in the U.S." Centers for Disease Control and Prevention.
www.cdc.gov/rabies/location/usa/index.html.

"Industry Statistics and Trends — Pet Ownership." American Pet

Products Association. **www.americanpetproducts.org/press _industrytrends.asp**.

Zoonotic diseases and owner health:

Centers for Disease Control and Prevention. **www.cdc.gov**.

"Zoonotic Diseases Tutorial." University of Wisconsin School of Veterinary Medicine. **www.vetmed.wisc.edu/pbs/zoonoses**.

Motooka, Masahiko, Hiroto Koike, Tomoyuki Yokoyama, and Nell L Kennedy. "Effect of dog-walking on autonomic nervous activity in senior citizens." The Medical Journal of Australia. **www.mja.com.au/public/issues/184_02_160106/mot10618_fm .html**.

Neal, Rome. "Sniffing Out Seizures." CBS News. **www.cbsnews .com/stories/2003/09/17/earlyshow/contributors/debbyeturner/ main573776.shtml**.

Other

"How Pet Microchipping Works." HowStuffWorks. **www.how stuffworks.com/pets/pet-travel/pet-microchip.htm**.

Keck, William. "Bob Barker is 'delighted' that spay-neuter phrase will stay." USA Today. **www.usatoday.com/life/television/ news/2007-07-24-barker-phrase_N.htm**.

Golden, Lori. "Protecting Animals Is More Than A Game For 'The Price Is Right' Host." The Pet Press. **www.thepetpress-la .com/articles/bobbarker.htm**.

Zollinger, Sue Ann. "Why Dogs Turn In Circles Before Lying Down." Indiana Public Media. **http://indianapublicmedia.org/amomentofscience/turning-circles-lying**.

Author's Bio

Jackie Sonnenberg is a Carthage College graduate who holds a bachelor's degree in English with an emphasis in creative writing. She has a history of writing experience, including publishing fiction in print and online in her teens and being a staff reporter for the local newspaper. Her work has appeared in *Echic, Kirby, The Daily Herald, Starpulse.com, eHow, BeepCentral,* and *Midwest Business*. This is her third published book.

She is an animal lover whose pet experience includes raising a pooch of her own, working at pet stores, serving as a pet sitter, and even volunteering to help find homes for a litter of kittens.

She currently is a reporter in Chicago covering business, technology, media, politics, and going green in the news, as well as for the Examiner Chicago edition writing about books and literature. She is a member of the Society of Children's Book Writers and Illustrators and has more fiction works in her plans.

Index